DIRECTORY

— OF THE —

CITY OF PLACERVILLE

AND TOWNS OF

UPPER PLACERVILLE, EL DORADO, GEORGETOWN,

AND COLOMA,

CONTAINING

A HISTORY OF THESE PLACES,

NAMES OF THEIR INHABITANTS, AND EVERYTHING
APPERTAINING TO A COMPLETE DIRECTORY.

TOGETHER WITH A

BUSINESS DIRECTORY.

By THOMAS FITCH & CO.

PLACERVILLE REPUBLICAN PRINTING OFFICE,
(Sebastopol Hall, Old Court House.)
1862.

Notice

In many older books, foxing (or discoloration) occurs and, in some instances, print lightens with wear and age. Reprinted books, such as this, often duplicate these flaws, notwithstanding efforts to reduce or eliminate them. The pages of this reprint have been digitally enhanced and, where possible, the flaws eliminated in order to provide clarity of content and a pleasant reading experience.

Placerville Republican:

PUBLISHED EVERY THURSDAY MORNING, BY
THOMAS FITCH & CO.

(OFFICE, IN SEBASTOPOL HALL.)

Terms of the Placerville Republican:

Single copy, one year	$5 00
Single copy, six months	3 00
Single copy, three months	1 50
Single copy, one month	50

INVARIABLY IN ADVANCE.

Rates for Advertising:

One square, first insertion	$3 00
Each subsequent insertion	1 00
Five lines, or less, first insertion	1 50
Each subsequent insertion	50

☞ For longer periods, and to regular advertisers, a liberal discount from the above rates will be made. ☞ Transient Advertisements must be paid for in advance.

A SUPERIOR JOB PRINTING OFFICE

Is connected with the Establishment, and every variety of Job Work will be executed at reasonable rates, and with the utmost neatness and dispatch.

AGENTS OF THE REPUBLICAN.

C. A. CRANE, Northwest corner Washington and Sansome streets, Government Building, up stairs, San Francisco.

H. S. HULBURD is authorized to solicit subscriptions, advertisements, etc.

D. C. HUMPHREYS is authorized to act as our Traveling Agent, to receive subscriptions, advertisements, etc.

HENRY JACOBS is our authorized Agent for Georgetown.

JOHN FOX is our Agent at Carson City, and will attend to all business for us faithfully and promptly.

PRINCIPAL CITIES IN CALIFORNIA.

From San Francisco

To Benicia 30
    Martinez 33
    Sacramento........... 125
    Stockton 227
    Petaluma............. 53
    Alviso 39
    San Mateo........... 21
    Redwood City........ 31
    San Jose 51
    Gilroy 85
    Santa Clara.......... 48
    Monterey............ 85
    San Juan............ 94
    San Diego 537

From Sacramento

To Nicolaus 26
    Bear River 29
    Dry Creek........... 37
    Marysville 44
    Tehama............. 119
    Red Bluffs........... 134
    Prairie House........ 145
    American House...... 160
    Carey's Ranch 169
    Shasta 220
    Iowa Hill............ 65
    Placerville........... 51
    Nevada.............. 69
    Auburn 38

From Marysville

To Charlie's Ranch...... 13
    Oroville 28
    Bidwell's Bar........ 32
    Honcut City 26
    Wyandot 25
    Natchez 30

To Buckeye 55
    Port Wine........... 75
    Onion Valley 81
    Forest City.......... 58
    Downieville........... 66
    Rough and Ready..... 32
    Grass Valley......... 36
    Nevada.............. 40

From Stockton

To Spring Valley........ 40
    Campo Seco.......... 46
    Mokelumne Hill...... 49
    Murphy's Camp...... 71
    Mammoth Tree Grove. 86
    Jamestown 71
    Sonora 75
    Columbia............ 81

From Placerville

To Folsom.............. 28
    Clarksville........... 21
    El Dorado........... 4
    Diamond Springs..... 2½
    Coloma 8
    Georgetown 12
    Uniontown 11
    Cold Springs......... 6
    Grizzly Flat.......... 23
    Wild Cat Bar........ 20
    Sportsman's Hall..... 12
    Crippen's............ 26
    Strawberry Valley.... 49
    Hawley's 60
    Genoa............... 85
    Carson City.......... 99
    Silver City........... 112
    Gold Hill............ 115
    Virginia City 117

PUBLISHERS' INTRODUCTION.

THE PUBLISHERS present this volume to their patrons, confident that it will form a valuable historical contribution, an efficient advertising medium, and a complete representative of the business and permanent population of PLACERVILLE, Upper Placerville, El Dorado, Georgetown and Coloma.

It is, of course, impossible to attain entire accuracy in a work of this description; but, as far as laborious and careful effort can accomplish such a result, they believe it has been achieved.

As the *first* Directory ever published in El Dorado County, this work will possess a peculiar interest.

THOMAS FITCH & CO.

EXPLANATION.

A slight error occurs in the History of Placerville, which was not discovered until after the work was in the binders' hands. The *soubriquet* of "Hangtown" was applied to Placerville not from the hanging of "Irish Dick," in 1850, but from the summary execution of the two Frenchmen and the Spaniard, who were hung in 1849, and not in 1854, as stated on page 11. No hanging, by a mob, has occurred here since 1850.

PART I.

—

PLACERVILLE.

HISTORY OF PLACERVILLE.

THE City of Placerville, the county seat of El Dorado County, California, is situated on the banks of Hangtown Creek, in a small valley in the Sierra Nevada mountains, in latitude 38° 43′ 40′ North, and longitude 120° 47′ West. Its altitude is 1,175 feet above the level of the sea, notwithstanding which it is never very cold in Winter, and snow seldom rests on the ground more than a day or two, as the city is protected from cold winds by the surrounding hills; these hills, however, tend to make the place very hot in midsummer, the thermometer sometimes indicating a temperature as high as 100 to 106° Fahrenheit, in the shade. Its topography secures it from much danger by floods. During the first month of the present year, a month more inclement and stormy than ever before known, the barometer was from 27:51 to 20:30 inches. The average hight for the month, 27:99 inches; temperature, at the same time, 46°. The amount of rain for the season was as follows: For the month of November, 8:15 inches; December, 21:05 inches; January, 34 inches—making, in all, 63:2 inches of rain during the three months named.

"Hangtown Creek," so famous throughout the State from its association with valuable gold mining and auriferous bed, derives its name from the early name of Placerville, through which it runs, and divides, as the Tiber does Rome. It is not an inconsiderable stream, especially in the rainy season. During the remarkable season just passed, it expanded to the magnitude of a river, and, by its sudden and temporary importance, caused some damage, but created no general alarm.

It soon subsided, however, into its proper channel, and will, until next season, continue to grow less each day. It has its source at the foot of Smith's Flat, about two miles East of the city, and is fed on its way by streams from Oregon, Cedar and other ravines adjacent to town. It loses itself in Weber Creek, about a mile and a-half West of the city. Weber Creek runs into the South Fork of the American River, which, in turn, unites with the Sacramento River.

The *soubriquet* of "Hangtown," by which Placerville was at one time only known, and which is now not unfrequently applied to it, had its origin in the hanging, by a mob, in October, 1850, of a desperado named Richard Crone, but known to the community by the *nom de plume* of "Irish Dick." The fellow was but a boy, hardly more than twenty-one years of age, and came across the Plains, from St. Louis, in one of the very first trains, in the capacity of a cook. He was of small stature, and more noticeable because of his *outre* attire, a wide and peculiar mouth, and large protruding teeth. He took to gambling as a profession, and showed, by his skill and pluck, that he was not unsuited for a business which, especially at that time, was a most hazardous calling. Like his fellows, he never went unarmed, and, like them, would not hesitate to use his weapons when he deemed it would aid his cause to do so. He soon made himself well known throughout the camps now included in El Dorado county, but honored "Hangtown" most generally with his presence. One night, while in the El Dorado Saloon (where now stands the Cary House), he stabbed, and almost instantly killed, an emigrant just arrived, mistaking him, it was said, for some one else whom he designed murdering, for some fancied offence. The murdered man had a brother in town, who resolved that "Irish Dick" should die. In this determination the town concurred. Dick was taken from the place where the officers of the law had stationed him, into the main street, and tried by a jury of citizens, in the presence of excited thousands, who had collected together from the surrounding country. The verdict was "guilty," and so soon as it was pronounced, the condemned was pushed from the temporary platform whereon he and the sheriff and extemporized court had sat, and hurried along with the crowd, towards the Plaza, where preparations were made for his execution. At this point the mob were told that a sick man was in a house near by, and that the uproar seriously troubled him. The crowd, at once, returned down Main street, and up to what is now Coloma street, to a large oak, near where is now the Presbyterian parsonage. Meanwhile, Sheriff "Bill" Rogers, and Alex. Hunter and John Clark, constables of the town, fought desperately for the possession of the prisoner, but, against the determined multitude, they were powerless. Throughout this terrible ordeal, "Dick," with a physical courage truly wonderful, conducted himself with the utmost coolness. When placed under the tree, with the rope around his neck, he begged the privilege of climbing upon the tree, and leaping from the fatal branch. But this was denied him, and he was jerked up by strong and willing hands, and was soon a dangling corpse.

The next and last fatal exercise of power by Judge Lynch was in 1854, when two Frenchmen and a Spaniard were hung by a mob, to an oak tree, at the corner of Main and Coloma streets, the stump of which is now covered by the store of Bye & Stewart. The victims had been arrested for highway robbery, on the Georgetown road. While being tried by a jury of citizens for this offence, and while it was doubtful what penalty should be inflicted on them, an officer from one of the lower counties arrived, in search of the perpetrators of a horrible murder in his section. On seeing the men being tried here for robbery, he at once recognized two of them as the murderers for whom he sought, and made the fact known. This, at once, settled their fate. Death was decreed as their verdict, and the sentence was carried out immediately, at the place and in the manner mentioned. Since that time Judge Lynch has been deposed (let us hope forever) in this region, nor has any one suffered the death penalty, except two Indians, for the murder of an Irishman named Gay, in 1861.

But other killing was done in Placerville, as elsewhere throughout the State, in those early and reckless times, when men had only in view the procurement of gold, which they squandered with more ease than they obtained it, and when established law had not yet assumed its sway. Among the offences of this nature, one is just now called to our recollection, from the fact that its author, only a few days since, met with a violent death, in Virginia City, at the hands of a constable named Williams, towards whom he cherished a demoniac hatred, and against whose life he had made threats. We allude to Bill Brown, who, in 1854, without provocation, entered a saloon on Main street, near Coloma, and so stabbed the barkeeper in the abdomen that his bowels protruded, and the poor fellow almost immediately died. The indignation was great; and, had it not been for the vigilance and determination of the authorities, Brown would have received summary and immediate punishment. Of his guilt there was not a shadow of doubt, but his counsel obtained postponement, and finally a change of venue, and when, at last, the culprit was brought to trial, the most important witnesses were found to have left the country, and could not be found. Enough was legally made against him to warrant his being sent to the State Prison for three years. After the expiration of his sen-

tence he crossed the mountains to Washoe, where he took the
life of a man called "Frenchy," but for this he was not pun-
ished, it appearing that the act was somewhat justifiable, and
that the loss of "Frenchy" was not a public calamity. And
now Brown, himself, is dead—a victim to that lawless violence
of which he was a prominent disciple.

Like nearly all towns in California, Placerville has not been
exempt from the ravages of the fire-fiend. From this cause
it suffered terribly in 1856. On the fifteenth of April, in that
year, the lower portion was laid in ruins by fire, which broke
out in Sacramento street, reducing to poverty, in the course
of a few hours, many who had before been rich. The victims
were nearly all hotel keepers, and included W. M. Cary, now
the popular and successful host of the Cary House, then of the
Placer Hotel. But, on the sixth of July, of the same year,
the town was completely laid in ashes by fire—scarcely a house
was saved, and lives were lost. And nothing better displays
the recuperative resources of the place than that Placerville
rose again, Phœnix-like, the brighter from its ashes, and is
still rising in extent, population, wealth, importance and sta-
bility, and having for its motto "Excelsior!"

Placerville was first incorporated as a city in the year 1853.
It now contains a population of about 5,000 souls, and is
steadily on the increase. A great impetus was given to its
growth and business by the rich mineral discoveries in Nevada
Territory, most of the travel to and from Virginia City pass-
ing through Placerville. A railroad to connect the city with
the Sacramento Valley Railroad, thirty miles distant, has been
projected and surveyed, and will probably be commenced in a
few months. One has also been projected to tide-water on the
San Joaquin river, and one across the mountains through

Johnson's Pass to Nevada Territory, there to connect with the great Atlantic and Pacific Railroad.

There are over two hundred business houses, some doing a large jobbing trade. There are several blocks of fire-proof brick buildings. Two fire-proof lava front engine houses, one of which (Neptune) contains a fine library, of over five hundred volumes The Court House, Churches, Odd Fellows' and Masons' Halls, Theater, etc., are all handsome and substantial edifices.

There is one daily and three weekly newspapers now published in Placerville. A large iron foundry, soap factory, carriage factory, blacksmith, wheelwright and other shops give employment to many mechanics.

The town of Upper Placerville, about one-fourth of a mile distant is a flourishing suburb, not at present included in the city limits. It has no peculiar history distinct from Placerville, and, with the progress of population, will eventually become a part of it.

COURTS.

District Court, Eleventh Judicial District.

B. F. Myers......................................Judge
Thos. B. Patten...................................Clerk

Regular terms commence on the second Mondays of February and May and third Mondays of August and November.

County Court.

James Johnson....................................Judge
Thos. B. Patten..................................Clerk

Regular terms commence on first Mondays of January, May and September.

Court of Sessions.

James Johnson..................................Judge
Geo. W. Stout and Hiram Falk...........Associate Judges
Thos. B. Patten...................................Clerk

Regular terms commence on first Mondays of March, July and November.

Probate Court.

James Johnson..................................Judge
Thos. R. Patten..................................Clerk

Regular terms first Monday of each month.

Justices' Court.

John Bush...................Office, Main st., near Coloma
G. W. Stout............................Upper Placerville

County Representatives.

Senators—A. St. C. Denver, O. Harvey.
Members of Assembly—Seneca Dean, J. Frasier, J. H. Dennis, H. G. Parker.

County Officers.

County Judge............................James Johnson
District Attorney..........................John Hume
Sheriff.......................................Alex. Hunter
County Clerk..........................Thomas B. Patten
County Collector........................J. M. Reynolds
County Recorder.......................Stephen Willetts
County Treasurer..........................J. L. Perkins
County Assessor.........................Geo. McDonald
Public Administrator.....................W. E. Gaylord
County Surveyor............................Hugh Barker
Superintendent Common Schools.............M. A. Lynde
County Coroner.........................W. Eichelroth

Township Officers.

Big Bar Township—Road Overseer, James Evans; Justices of the Peace, E. D. Roach, A. W. Haskell; Constables, Joseph Corlis, John Tearney.

Coloma Township—Road Overseer, D. A. McFee; Justices of the Peace, George A. Douglass, William Gibbs; Constables, John Curtis, Pat. Freeney.

Cosumnes Township—Road Overseer, E. H. Richardson; Justices of the Peace, J. S. Lock, John Ensey; Constables, M. N. Renick, C. F. Peck.

Diamond Springs Township—Road Overseer, C. P. Young; Justices of the Peace, John Fleming, Alex. Seisbuttle; Constables, Jno. W. Keyser, Joseph R. Smith.

Georgetown Township—Road Overseer, A. W. Partes; Justices of the Peace, E. L. Smith, J. R. Spaulding; Constables, James Hussey, T. J. Correll.

Greenwood Township—Road Overseer, Geo. E. Freeman; Justices of the Peace, F. A. Hornblower, J. I. Moore; Constables, Thos. F. Lewis, J. H. Smith.

Kelsey Township—Road Overseer, R. Demuth; Justices of the Peace, L. Borneman, H. Rolkey; Constables, James H. Hughes, Johnson Odeneal.

Mountain Township—Road Overseer, William Knox; Justices of the Peace, William Knox, O. S. Palmer; Constables, J. Smith, J. H. Rader.

Mud Springs Township—Road Overseer, N. Gilmore; Justices of the Peace, James McCormick, Hiram Falk; Constables, C. T. Roussin, Jos. E. Simmons.

Placerville Township—Road Overseer, John Miller; Justices of the Peace, John Bush, G. W. Stout; Constables, A. Simonton, R. K. Emmerson.

Salmon Falls Township—Road Overseer, Charles Green; Justices of the Peace, R. K. Berry, Sam. Smith; Constables, Nathan Oakes, Samuel Atkinson.

White Oak Township—Road Overseer, Pat. Lyman; Justices of the Peace, George Bramall, B. Rodahan; Constables, J. S. Nowlan, E. Brandon.

CITY GOVERNMENT.

THOMAS B. WADE,............................ Mayor
George M. Condee, Mike Borowsky, J. M. Reynolds, W. H.
  Cooper, C. T. Murphy and D. L. Munson, Aldermen.
C. E. Chubbuck,............. Clerk and *ex Officio* Assessor
J. A. McDougald,...........Marshal and *ex Officio* Collector
John Hume,................................City Attorney
J. J. Reynolds and John D. Van Eaton,.........Policemen

FIRE DEPARTMENT.

CHIEF ENGINEER ....
First Assistant Engineer ....William McBrien
Second Assistant Engineer.................John J. Cullen
President Board of Delegates.................Alex. Hunter
Vice President Board of Delegates.......George M. Condee
Secretary Board of Delegates............Thomas B. Wade
Treasurer Fire Department ....Aaron Kahn
Trustees.....F. F. Barss, Geo. M. Condee, J. McT. Pierson

CHURCHES.

Methodist Episcopal Church, corner Main street and Cedar
  Ravine—Rev. J. W. Ross, Pastor.
St. Patrick's Church (Roman Catholic), Sacramento street—
  Rev. J. Largan, Pastor.
Presbyterian Church, Coloma street—Rev. J. McMonagle,
  Pastor.
Protestant Episcopal Church, at Court House—Rev. C. C.
  Peirce, Pastor.
Hebrew Synagogue, Cottage street—H. C. Glauber, Rabbi.

SOCIETIES.

MASONS.

El Dorado Lodge, No. 26, meets at Masonic Hall on the Monday of or next preceding the Full Moon of each month.

I. S. Titus.........................Worshipful Master
C. E. Chubbuck ....Secretary

Palmyra Lodge (U. D.) meets in the new Hall, Upper Placerville, on Tuesday nights next preceding the Full Moon of each month.

James McBeth .... Worshipful Master
Benjamin Meacham........................Secretary

St. James Royal Arch Chapter, No. 16, meets in Masonic Hall, on the evenings of the first and third Wednesday of each month.

Aaron Kahn...............Most Excellent High Priest
I. S. Titus...............................Secretary

Sierra Nevada Council, No. 40, of Royal and Select Masters, holds stated meetings on the evenings of the first Tuesday of each month, in Masonic Hall.

L. W. Rumsey............................. T. I. M.
I. S. Titus ... .Recorder

El Dorado Commandery, No. 4, meets at Masonic Hall on the first Thursday of every month.

L. W. Rumsey.................Excellent Commander
I. S. Titus............................... Recorder

*** Masonic Hall, Main street, over Aaron Kahn's store. Palmyra Lodge meets in the New Hall on Main street, Upper Placerville.

I. O. OF O. F.

Morning Star Lodge, No. 20, meets every Saturday evening, at Odd Fellows' Hall, on Stony Point.

McK. Burton............................ Noble Grand
A. Simonton...............................Secretary

Franklin Lodge, No. 74, meets every Wednesday evening, at Odd Fellows' Hall.

August Erdsinger.......................Noble Grand
William Eichelroth........................ Secretary

Zeta Encampment, No. 5, meets in Odd Fellows' Hall, on the evenings of the second and fourth Tuesday of each month.

A. A. Van Voorhies......................Chief Priest
G. W. Howlett .... Scribe

TEMPERANCE ORDERS.

Upper Placerville Division Sons of Temperance meets in Temperance Hall, Upper Placerville, every Wednesday evening, at 7 o'clock.

Independent Order of Good Templars meet every Friday evening. at 7 o'clock, in Temperance Hall, Upper Placerville.

HEBREW BENEVOLENT SOCIETY.

The Hebrew Benevolent Society of Placerville meets on the first Sunday of every month, in the Hall of Hope Hook and Ladder Company.

A. Kahn................................... President
A. Haas................................... Secretary

EL DORADO COUNTY MEDICAL SOCIETY.

J. R. Edwards............................. President
I. S. Titus...............................Secretary

ABBREVIATIONS.

R. for residence; bet. for between; st. for street; bds. for boards; initial letters for points of the compass; s. for side; Ced. Rav. for Cedar Ravine; prop'r for proprietor; h., house.

PLACERVILLE DIRECTORY.

A

Adriatic Restaurant, Peter Fox, prop'r. s. s. Main st., opposite Coloma;

Alderson Anne, prop'r Alderson's Exchange, Sacramento st.;

Alderson George, miner, boards at Alderson's Exchange;

Alderson Thomas, miner, boards at Alderson's Exchange;

Alderson Richard, saloon keeper, Sacramento street;

Allen John, miner; house, Cedar Ravine;

Allen James C., wheelwright, with Orris, Main street;

Allsworth Benjamin, miner; house, Sacramento street, e. s., above Chamberlain;

Alsberg Sigmund, cigars and confectionery, n. s. Main street;

Alverson William, brick layer; house, Sacramento street;

ALVERSON STEPHEN H., blacksmith and wheelwright, n. s. Main, above Coloma st.; h., Sacramento street;

Alvomet ——, tailor, Benham Place;

Alverez Ferdinand, packer, Chapal street;

Anundson Thomas, boot maker, with M. Bottger;

ANDARS ADOLPH, proprietor Globe Hotel, n. s. Main st., opposite Sacramento;

ANDERSON J. M., of Hernandez & Anderson; house, south side of Main street, above Cedar Ravine;

Andrews Edmund, tinner, with I. H. Nash, bds. Cary House;

Alverez Jose A., packer, Chapel street;

Anzer George, boot maker, with G. A. F. Rendle ;
Armstrong & Hunger, butchers, s. s. Main, near Sacramento;
Armstrong William (of A. & H.); boards at Orleans Hotel;
AUDITOR COUNTY—office, Court House ;
Augusta C. H., barber, with S. W. Huff;
Ardary John, Gas Works ; house, Coloma street;
Ardary James, Gas Works; house, Coloma street;
ARVIDSSON & CO., C. J., jewelers and gunsmiths, north
    side Main street, between Coloma street and the Plaza;
Arvidsson C. J. (of C. J. A. & Co.); house, n. s. Cottage st. ;
Arvidsson A. C. (of C. J. A. & Co.); boards with C. J. A. ;
Averill Frank, blacksmith, with S. H. Alverson.

B

Badillo Jesus, packer; house, Chapel street ;
Baker Silas, barber, with J. Johnson ;
Baldwin C., painter, with Packer, Main street ;
Baldwin William, waiter at Cary House ; house, High street ;
Ballard J. Q. A., barkeeper Oasis Saloon ;
Balensuela Miguel, packer ; house, Chapel street ;
Bamberger S., clothing merchant, n. s. Main st., near Plaza ;
Bank John, cook at Hope and Neptune Restaurant;
Barman Isaac, of P. Silberman & Co.; bds. at Cary House ;
Barnes ——. printer, boards at Mountjoy House;
Barnes Charles W., clerk with Hunt & Chace, Main street ;
Barrett Benjamin, clerk at Armstrong & Hunger's ;
Barrett Charles, boards with Pierson, Main street;
BARSS F. F., watchmaker and jeweler, n. s. Main street,
    bet. Coloma st. and Plaza; house, e. s. Coloma street;
Bartram W., lumber yard, s. s. Main st.; bds. Cary House ;
Bartlett Cyrus, teacher Public School ; house, Bedford avenue;
Barton H., blacksmith, at Orris', Main street ;

Baylor J., of Baylor & Mason, Empire Stable, Main street ;
BAYLOR & MASON, Empire Stable, Main street;
Beach T., cook at Cedar Ravine Hotel, Main street ;
Bee F. A., Coloma street ;
Beckman Eugene, chemist, German Drug Store, Main st.;
    boards at Placer Hotel;
Becker S. S., blacksmith, Main street; house, Cedar Ravine ;
Beckman Henry, miner, boards with Hays, Sacramento st.;
Beck Caroline, washing, Cottage street, near Coloma ;
Begeman John, laborer; house, Pacific street ;
Behever Frank, barber, with John Vantine ;
BEKEART FRANK, gunsmith, Main st., near the Theater ;
Bell George, tinner, with I. H. Nash ; house, e. s. Coloma st.;
Bell Mrs. Mary, west side Bedford avenue ;
Bell William, west side Bedford avenue ;
BENNETT & CRIPPEN, livery stable, north side Main st.,
    near Sacramento ;
Bennett William, of Bennett & Crippen ;
Bennett O. S., barkeeper, with John O'Donnell ;
Bennett William, hostler, Canal street ;
Bergantz Jacob, drayman ; house, Benham street;
Bernathowitz Leo, of Pebelie & Co.; boards at Cary House ;
Bertrand Baschier, barkeeper, with Anne Radignet ;
Bigelow E., cook, Orleans Hotel ;
Bird William, laborer, Pacific street ;
Bird John. laborer, Cedar Ravine ;
Binswanger L., fruits, etc.; house, near Mill street ;
Bishop F. A., Civil Engineer, office South Fork Canal Co.;
    boards at Cary House ;
Blair John, teamster ; house, Cedar Ravine ;
BLACK R. H., Court House Exchange, north side Main st.,
    near the Court House ;
Blanchard H., steward, Mountjoy House ;

Blanchard G. G., lawyer, corner Main and Coloma streets;
BLOCH A., dry goods, north side Main street, between Coloma street and the Plaza;
Blood J., carpenter; boards with J. Shira, Main street;
Blouf Felix, bootmaker, with W. T. Henson;
Boarigo Peres, miner; Reservoir street;
Boldrini Fortunato, saloon; s. s. Main st., between Plaza and Bedford avenue;
Bolton ——, painter; boards at Mountjoy House;
Boker S. S., blacksmith, Cedar Ravine;
BOROWSKY MICHAEL, billiard saloon, Plaza, over post office; house, e. s. Coloma street;
Boop Jno. D., lumber agent, Cedar Ravine; house, w. s. Bedford avenue;
Bottger Geo., bootmaker, n. s. Main st., next to Mountjoy;
Booth John, plasterer; house. Cedar Ravine;
Booth George, brickmason; house, Cedar Ravine;
Bowyer George, miner; house, Cedar Ravine;
Borugon Jos., shoemaker, Sacramento st., w. s., near Main;
Bradbury T. L., carpenter, Center street;
Brady G., laborer; boards at Esmeralda House, Main street;
BRADSHAW W. M. & CO., books and stationery, north side Main street, between the Plaza and Coloma street;
Bradshaw W. M. (of W. M. B. & Co.); boards at Sierra Nevada House;
Bradley L. L., speculator; with D. W. Levan;
Brill Abraham, speculator; with Hunter & Lynch;
Brondley Joseph, blacksmith, west side Sacramento street;
Brice Eliza, Main street, south side, near turnpike;
Brown James M., waiter, Cary House;
Brown W. D., bowling alley, Main street;
Brown J. R., carpenter, west side Bedford avenue;
Brown William, laborer, Main street, west side;

Brown W. H., livery stable, n. s. Main st., opposite Orleans ;

Brayman William, packer ;

Brewery Placerville, Benham street ;

Brewery Mountain, head of Court alley ;

Brazee Francis, bootmaker, south side Main street, between
Plaza and Bedford avenue ; boards at Orleans Hotel ;

Brownell H. H., north side Main street, between Coloma and
Plaza, up stairs ;

Bruce Phebe, Main street, near turnpike ;

BRUSIE & RUSSELL, bowling saloon, south side Main
street, above the Plaza ;

Brusic James, groceries and provisions, south side Main st.,
on the Plaza ; house, Washington street ;

Bryant J. G., groceries and provisions ; bds. at Mountjoy ;

Budde Frank, city laundry, Center street ;

Buller Frank, teamster, Benham street ;

Buoker Dan'l C. metropolitan bathing saloon, s. s. Main st.;

Burnham Martin, clerk, with L. B. Richardson & Co., boards
at Cary House ;

Bullett William, at Mountain Brewery ;

Burtt L. D. packer, boards at Cary House ;

BURNS & McBRIDE, groceries and provisions, north side
Main street, on the Plaza ;

Burns W. S. (of B. & McB.); house Main st., near Ced. Rav.;

Burns Sarah E., cigars, n. s. Main st., near Cedar Ravine ;

Bush John, justice, s. s. Main st., opp. Coloma st., up stairs ;

Butts Jas., barber, with J. B. Jenkins, bds. with Mrs. Turk ;

Butler Thomas, teamster, west side Bedford avenue ;

Butler Orris, teamster, west side Bedford avenue ;

BYE & STEWART, grocers, n. s. Main st., near Coloma st.;

Bye F. W. (of Bye & Stewart); boards at Cary House ;

C

Cading Henry, miner, Main street, near toll gate;
CAGWIN & CO., H. A., dry goods and clothing, south side
    Main street, near Plaza;
Cagwin H. A. (of H. A. C. & Co.); house e. s. Bedford av.;
Cagwin H. A. Jr., clerk, with H. A. C. & Co., bds. H. A. C.;
Cagwin O. D., clerk, with H. A. C. & Co., bds. H. A. C.;
Cagwin J. A., house, Bedford avenue;
CALIFORNIA STATE AND OVERLAND TELEGRAPH
    CO., northwest corner of Main and Coloma sts., up stairs;
Campbell Robert, house, Cedar Ravine;
Campbell John, miner, house Cedar Ravine;
Campbell Daniel, miner, house, Cedar Ravine;
Campbell John, teamster, boards at Cedar Ravine Hotel.
Canton J. P., deputy collector, boards at Cary House;
Canavan E. J., clerk, with G. P. Morrill; bds. at Mountjoy;
Carrillo Francis, silversmith; house Chapel street;
Carndy George; house, east side Coloma street;
Carney Thomas, laborer; house Mill street, near Spring;
Carson E. B., under sheriff; house, west side Coloma street;
CARR & PALMER, attorneys, south side Main street, oppo-
    site Coloma street, up stairs;
Carr L. T. (of C. &. P.); house, east side Chamberlain street;
CARY HOUSE, south side Main street, opposite Coloma st.;
CARY & CULLEN, proprietors Cary House;
Cary W. M., of Cary & Cullen;
CARY HOUSE SALOON, W. M. Donahue, proprietor;
Case Wm., carpenter, with O. Taylor, Jr.; boards Canal st.;
Castano O., saloon, s. s. Main st., bet. Plaza and Bedford av.;
Castonia S., saloon, s. s. Main st., bet. Plaza and Bedford av.;
Castill M. packer; boards at Cary House;

Chace H. A. (of Hunt & Chace); boards at Mountjoy House;
Channell John H., miner ; house, Cedar Ravine ;
Chapman W. R., deputy sheriff; boards at Cary House;
Chandler A. S , cigars, Oasis Saloon ; house, Center street;
Cherry David W., blacksmith ; house, west side Coloma st.;
Chesterfield ——, barber; house, Center street ;
Chestnut John C., clerk, with J. M. Douglass;
Chichester D. W., at Bartram's lumber yard; bds. Cary House;
Child S. F., dentist. Mountjoy House ;
Christian E., blacksmith, with Orris, Main street ;
Chubbuck C. E., city clerk; house, west side Coloma street;
Chubbuck James, jeweler, Main street; house, Cottage street;
Church W., cook, at Mountjoy House ;
CLARK A., physician, city block, north side Main street,
    between Coloma street and Plaza, up stairs ;
Clark C., shoemaker, s. s. Main st., above Bedford avenue ;
Clark J., miner, Cedar Ravine ;
Claude H. G., with White & Metzler;
CLAYTON M. F., physician, north side Main street, near
    Cedar Ravine ;
Clees J. P. (of Weymouth & Clees); boards at Cary House ;
Coffey W. H., clerk, with W. M. Donahue; bds. Cary House ;
Cohen Jacob, clerk, with A. Bloch ;
Cohn Edward, tailor, south side Main street, on the Plaza;
Cook William, laborer, Benham Place ;
COOKE & TITUS, physicians, northwest corner Main and
    Coloma streets, up stairs ;
Cooke John, (of Cooke & Titus); boards at Cary House ;
Cook Edward C., clerk, with Burns & McBride; boards at
    Cedar Ravine Hotel;
Colby William G., builder, Cedar Ravine ;
Colliboo Frank, west side Bedford avenue;
Cole Richard, printer ; house, west side Bedford avenue;

Collins F., clerk, with I. H. Nash ; house, Pleasant Hill ;
Condee George M., insurance agent; house, e. s. Coloma st.;
Confidence Engine House, n. s. Main st., near Stony Point;
Congdon George, teamster ; house, east side Sacramento st.;
Conway John, livery stable, n. s. Main st.; bds. at Orleans ;
Cooper William H., east side Sacramento street ;
Cooper Emma, n. s. Main st., bet. Bedford av. and Ced. Rav.;
Cory Nathaniel, cabinetmaker, with C. L. Crisman ; boards
    at Mountjoy House ;
COUNTY CLERK'S OFFICE, Court House ;
Cordell John, carpenter, west side Bedford avenue ;
Cottrell M. L., saloon keeper, Main street ;
CRANDALL J. B., stage proprietor ; house, west side
    Coloma street ;
Crippin Calvin, (of Bennett & Crippin); h., e. s. Bedford av.;
Crippin Charles, teamster ; house, west side Bedford avenue ;
Crippin J. J., teamster ; house, east side Bedford avenue ;
Crippin John, laborer ; house, west side Bedford avenue ;
Crippin J. W., laborer ; house, west side Bedford avenue ;
CRISMAN C. L., furniture, north side Main street, near
    Stony Point;
Crowder J. J., driver for P. S. Co.; boards at Cary House ;
Crowell Charles, driver for P. S. Co.; boards at Cary House;
Cruch B. J., miner; boards at Orleans Hotel ;
Crumry Johanna, Cedar Ravine ;
Cullen J. W., of Cary & Cullen ;
Cullen J. J., jeweler, with J. M. Seeley ; house, Cottage st.;

D

Daggett W. C., of Harvey, Daggett & Co.;
Dalton John, ranchman, Cedar Ravine ;
Danforth C. W., tinner, with I. H. Nash ; boards at Cedar
    Ravine Hotel ;

Dascomb Thomas R., miner; house, east side Sacramento st.;
Dascomb George, miner; house, east side Sacramento street;
DAVIS C. E., dentist, north side Main st. near Cedar Ravine;
Davis S., teamster, west side Bedford avenue;
Davis Hannah, millinery, north side Main st., near Coloma.
Davison Thomas, butcher, with C. Etzel; bds. National Res.;
Davidson M. N., carpenter; boards at Orleans Hotel;
Day E. C., blacksmith, with G. W. Farr; bds. at Orleans;
Dench J. W., harnessmaker, at Phipps', Sacramento street;
Dempsey Christoper, Fulton Market, south side Main street,
    between Plaza and Bedford avenue;
Derham James, porter, Cary House;
Dewitt Lemuel, ditch-tender, S. F. Canal; bds. with J. Shira;
DIAS & GLAUBER, forwarding and commission merchants,
    Coloma street;
Dias A. H. L. (of D. & G.); h., Cottage st., near Coloma;
Dickerhoff Martin, miner; house, Cedar Ravine;
Dierer George, saloon, south side Main st., on the Plaza;
DONAHUE W. M., wholesale liquor dealer, north side Main
    street, opposite the Theater;
Donnelly John, bakery and fruits, north side Main street, near
    Cedar Ravine;
Donnelly Patrick, laborer; boards with John Donnelly;
Doyle Michael, bartender, at Murphy's, Main street;
Dupey James, house, south side Union street;
DOUGLASS J. M., banker and gold dust buyer, south side
    Main street, next to Cary House; boards at Cary House;
Duden C. W., deputy recorder; house, Canal street;
DUNBAR J. W., drayman, west side Bedford avenue;
Duffit George, New York House, Main street;
Dunn Daniel, blacksmith, Sacramento street, near Main st.;
Dunn Thomas, blacksmith, Sacramento street, near Main st.;
Dunlap John W., with W. M. Bradshaw & Co.

D

EASTMAN & WILLIAMS, attorneys, south side Main st.,
    next to Cary House, up stairs ;
Ebens John, shoemaker ; house, Pacific street ;
Ebernarde Antoine, cook, at National Restaurant ;
Edward Nancy, washing, Cary alley ;
Eichelroth William, county coroner, office, Mountjoy House ;
Eichelroth Wm, physician and surgeon, German drug store ;
Eidinger August, vegetables, west side Sacramento street ;
ELKUS L., merchant tailor, Main street, between Coloma
    street and Plaza ;
Ellis James, deputy collector ; house, east side Coloma street ;
Elliott John, workman, New York Hotel ;
Elliott Anderson, workman, New York Hotel ;
Elrick Scott, laborer, Cedar Ravine ;
Elstner M. R., boards at Mountjoy House ;
Ensminger S. C., packer, with Munson & Co.; boards at
    Mountjoy House ;
Esmeralda House, Main street, near Cedar Ravine ;
Etzel Conrad & Co., butchers, s. s. Main st., on the Plaza.

F

Fagan John, laborer ; house, Spring street ;
FAIRCHILD O. L. C., foreman Republican Office, boards at
    Cary House ;
Fairman John, barkeeper, with Loney ;
Farr George M., blacksmith and carriage maker, north side
    Main street, between the Plaza and Bedford avenue ;
Fechheimer L. W., book-keeper, with Landecker ;
Felschi R., laborer, Reservoir street ;
Fellman A., hostler for P. S. Co., boards at Cary House ;

Placerville Daily News.

THE PLACERVILLE NEWS is published every morning, (Mondays excepted) and furnished to City Subscribers at 25 cents per week, payable to the Carrier. Single copies, 10 cts. It will be forwarded to any part of the State, by Mail or Express, at $8 per annum, in advance; $5 for six months; $3 for three months.

JOB PRINTING!

The Publishers of the PLACERVILLE DAILY NEWS announce to their friends and the public that they are in possession of

A COMPLETE JOB PRINTING ESTABLISHMENT,

Comprising a great variety of NEW AND ATTRACTIVE TYPE, together with all the necessary appliances for the execution of the FINEST PRINTING—such as

CARDS, CHECKS,
CIRCULARS, BILLHEADS,
BALL TICKETS, POSTERS,
PROGRAMMES, LABELS, &c.,

Unsurpassed in workmanship, and on terms reasonable and satisfactory.

☞ Advertisements conspicuously inserted, at rates conformable with the cost of living, and every effort made to advance the interests of the advertiser.

☞ Office in Dorsey's Building (up stairs), Main street, Placerville.

GEORGE YARNELL & CO.,
Publishers and Proprietors,

Felton W. W., proprietor City Laundry :
Fenlyson James, clerk, with A. Haas ;
Ferman D., carpenter ; boards at Cedar Ravine Hotel ;
Ferry George T., packer ; boards at Cary House ;
Fink J. J., saloon, n. w. cor. Main st. and Bedford avenue ;
Fisher Daniel, saloon keeper, s. s. Main st., on the Plaza ;
Fisher Leonard, blacksmith for P. S. Co.; bds. at Cary House ;
Fiske L. C., real estate agent, east side Sacramento street ;
FITCH CHARLES A., SOAP MANUFACTURER, Cedar
    Ravine ;
FITCH GEORGE L., Cedar Ravine ;
FITCH & CO. THOMAS, publishers *Placerville Republican;*
Fitch Thomas, of Thos. Fitch & Co.; boards at Cary House ;
Flanagan Michael, of Walker & Flanagan ;
Fleming M. T., Mountjoy House ;
Flonae M., Center street ;
Foll John, butcher, with M. S. Metzler; house, Coloma st.;
Fonda A., west side Sacramento street ;
Forman Mrs. M., north side Main street ;
Fountain Caroline, milliner, Main street ;
Fowler T. S., carpenter, south side Main st., cor. Turnpike ;
FOX PETER, Adriatic Restaurant, Main street ;
FRANCIS G., clothing and furnishing goods, north side Main
    street, on the Plaza ; house, Cedar Ravine ;
Fratiger G., carpenter, Benham street ;
Freeharner J., miner, Pacific street;
Freeman George W., of Freeman & Lemon ;
Freeman & Lemon, proprietors Cedar Ravine Hotel ;
Fripp Miss Mary, Cedar Ravine ;
Fumerton J., of Geo. Yarnell & Co.; boards with Mrs. Cole ;
Furnish L. G., clerk, with M. Berowsky ;
Furness C. H., of Smith & Furness;
Fury H., laborer, Esmeralda House, Main street.

Gage S. T., packer; boards at Cary House;
Gardiner James, waiter at Cary House;
Gardner F. A., night-watch at Mountjoy House;
Garrett John R., clerk, with R. White;
Gas Works Placerville, Coloma street;
Ganson Albert, bricklayer; boards with J. Shira;
GELWICKS & JANUARY, *Mountain Democrat*, Coloma st.;
Gelwicks Daniel, of Gelwicks & January; house, Coloma st.;
Gentry A., speculator, Oasis saloon; house, e. s. Coloma st.;
Gellenheimer F., Mountain Brewery; house, Cary alley;
Gerham Michael, Mountain Brewery; house, Cary alley;
Germain Louis, tailor, Sacramento street;
GERMAN DRUG STORE, n. s. Main st., near Sacramento;
Gibbons John, packer; boards at Cary House;
Gilbert G. H., Daguerrean Gallery, north east corner Main
    and Coloma streets, up stairs;
Gilmore Robert, blacksmith for P. S. Co.; bds. at Cary House;
Gilnster William, carpenter; house, Mill street;
Glauber H., of Dias & Glauber, east side Coloma street;
Glass A., peddler, Mountjoy House;
Glass J., peddler, Mountjoy House;
Glenn Robert, printer, *Times* office; bds. at Orleans Hotel;
GLOBE HOTEL, Adolph Ardass, proprietor, Main street,
    opposite Sacramento;
GLYNN IRA, dentist, n. s. Main st., below Sacramento;
Goan ——, miner, Cedar Ravine;
Goldner Julius, of W. M. Bradshaw & Co.; h., Goldner st.;
Gomez Antonio, packer; house, Chapel street;
Gong Yong, teas, etc., Benham street;
Gormitzyora Charles, painter, east side Sacramento street;

Gray John, boards at Mountjoy House;

Grant P., Bella Union Saloon, Main street;

Grantham J. M., printer, *Democrat* office;

Green J. J., deputy sheriff; boards at Cary House;

Greeley O. F., clerk in Post Office; bds. with W. H. Rogers;

Green E., saloon, north side Main street;

Greeman John, tailor, with L. Elkus;

Gritzner A., boards at Mountjoy House;

Grotto Saloon, Anna Bradford, north side Main street;

Grover H. C., of Geo. Yarnell & Co.; h., w. s. Bedford av.;

Guild James, telegraph operator; boards with Mrs. Irvine;

Guidici Tereise, boarding house, Reservoir street;

Guidici F. E., laborer, boards with T. Guidici;

Guidici V. I., laborer, boards with T. Guidici.

H

HAAS A., dry goods, north side Main street, near the Plaza;
    house, west side Coloma street;

HAAS S. & CO., clothing, s. s. Main street, near the Plaza;

Hackett J. C., carpenter;

Halftermeyer Amand, Sebastopol Hall;

Hall H. C., clerk with H. A. Cagwin & Co., Main street;

Hall B. J., carpenter, Benham Place;

Hall ——, carpenter, Washington street;

Hamberger Jules, " Snug" Saloon, Coloma street;

Hammell Henry, Benham street;

HANAK & SESSER, hardware, Main st., opposite Coloma;

Hancock W. V., carpenter, boards at Cedar Ravine Hotel;

Harker W. B., boards at Mountjoy House;

Harmon F. H., notary public; boards at Orleans Hotel;

HARRIS S., books and stationery, Post Office building, on
    the Plaza; house, east side Bedford avenue;

Harris Louis, steward, Orleans Hotel;
Harris George, carpenter, County road;
HARRINGTON HIRAM, physician, w. s. Sacramento st.;
Hartmann George, miner, Benham street;
Hartmann John, miner, Benham street;
Harvey, Daggett & Co., liquor dealers, on the Plaza;
Harvey W. M., of Harvey, Daggett & Co.;
Harvey O., physician, City Block, north side Main street;
HASKELL, BECKER & SHEPHERD, wagon-wagers, Main
    street, near Cedar Ravine;
Haskell William, boards at Cedar Ravine Hotel;
Hawley B. F., miner;
Hawley C. H., miner;
Hayes James, waiter, Cary House;
Hay Henry, east side Sacramento street;
Hay Mrs. H., midwife, east side Sacramento street;
Headley Clinton, teamster, boards with J. Shira;
Henry A. C.; residence, Chamberlain street;
HENSON W. T., boots and shoes, south side Main st., above
    the Cary House; boards at Cary House;
HERNANDEZ & ANDERSON, books and stationery, n. s.
    Main street, on the Plaza;
Hernandez R. S., of H. & A., west side Coloma street;
Hescherd F., laborer, Main street;
Heusner Paul, St. Louis Hotel, Main street;
Hinckley Oliver, P. S. Co.'s stables; house, Chapel street;
Hickey James, laborer;
Hicks E. A., with Mike Borowsky; house, Main street;
Hicks William, Main street, north side;
Hierson A., clothing; boards at Mountjoy House;
Higgins James S., teamster, Cary alley;
Hilbert Charles, New York House, north side Main street;
Hill G., hostler, P. S. Co.'s stables; boards at Cary House;

Hill William, cook, Alderson's Exchange, Sacramento st.;
Hill William, laborer, boards with J. J. Reynolds;
Hill William H., speculator;
Hoffman C. B., driver for P. S. Co., boards at Cary House;
Hofmeister F., beer saloon, Main street, near Sacramento;
Hogsett Thomas, of Lacey & Hogsett, boards Cary House;
Hooker V. B., driver for P. S. Co., boards at Cary House;
Hook F., butcher, with Armstrong & Hunger, Main street;
Hooper William, steward, Orleans Hotel;
Hopkins L. B., miner, w. s. Coloma street, near Main;
HOPE AND NEPTUNE RESTAURANT, on the Plaza;
Hovolencia Jose, west side Sacramento street;
Howard L., bootblack, in Theater building, on the Plaza;
Howard Nicholas, bootblack, s. s. Main, near Sacramento st.;
Howard Daniel, miner, Bedford avenue;
Howland C., milliner, with Mrs. H. Irwin, Main street;
Huff William, barber, Main street; h., e. s. Coloma street;
Huff S. W., barber, on the Plaza; h., e. s. Coloma street;
Hughes M., harness maker, with A. A. Van Voorhies;
HUME & SLOSS, attorneys, north side Main st., between
    Coloma street and the Plaza;
Hume John, of H. & S.; house, east side Bedford avenue;
Hume J. B., deputy collector; house, Piety Hill;
Humphreys D. C., agent *Republican;* house, Spring street;
Hunger F., of Armstrong & Hunger; house, Main street;
HUNTER & LYNCH, Magnolia Saloon, south side of Main
    street, between Coloma street and the Plaza;
Hunter Alex., of H. & L., Sheriff, High street;
Hunter Mason, miner, Cedar Ravine;
Hunter Robert, clerk with Landecker; bds. Nat. restaurant;
HUNT & CHACE, grocers, on the Plaza, opp. Theater;
Hunt B. T., of Hunt & Chace;
Huron Louis, beer saloon, n. s. Main st., near Sacramento;

Hussey B. A., clerk with J. Brusie;
Hyers Robert, barber, Metropolitan Bath House;
Hyman William, steward, Orleans Hotel.

I

IRON FOUNDRY PLACERVILLE, Mead, Tasker & Co.,
    proprietors, foot of Mill street;
Irvine Alexander, Cottage street, near Coloma;
IRWIN MRS. A. E., millinery, north side Main street, bet.
    Coloma street and the Plaza.

J

Jackson ——, carpenter, east side Coloma street;
January W. A., of Gelwicks & January, e. s. Coloma street;
Jenkins J. B., barber, s. s. Main street, near Sacramento;
Jennings John, shoemaker, s. s. Main st., near Cedar Ravine;
Jennings Fletcher, shoemaker, bds. at Cedar Ravine Hotel;
Jewell G., of Munson & Jewell;
Johnson August, clerk with Richard Kiene;
Johnson J., barber, on the Plaza; house, Cottage street;
Johnson James, County Judge; house, new Turnpike road;
Johnson Jane, n. s. Main street;
Johnston W., hostler, Empire Stable, Main street;
JOHNS D. D., Oasis Saloon; house, High street;
Jones D. H., porter Wells, Fargo & Co.; bds. Cary House;
Jones Geo. F., of L. B. Richardson & Co.; h., Coloma street;
Jones Charles, miner; boards with J. Shira;
Jones John, cook at S. Murphy's, Main street;
Jones J., miner, Cedar Ravine;
Judge L., waiter at Adriatic Restaurant.

K

KAHN AARON, clothing, north side Main street, between Coloma st. and Plaza; h., Main st., below Sacramento ;

Keck H. D., cabinet maker, with C. L. Crisman ;

Keller Lew., auctioneer, with H. Louis & Co.;

KELLER L., proprietor Greyhound Saloon, Main street;

Kelley James, saloon, Main st., near Mountjoy House ;

Kelley William, at City Laundry ;

Kennedy R., teamster, Cedar Ravine ;

Kenney E. L., teamster, Cary alley ;

Kinn A., clerk with Wells, Fargo & Co.; bds. Cary House ;

Kerley J. C., printer, *Democrat* office ;

Keyser ——, miner, Pacific street ;

Kee Sin, tea merchant, Sacramento street ;

Kee Fi, provision dealer, Sacramento street;

Kiene R., saloon, Main st., near Sacramento ; h., Center st.;

Kibble, tailor, with L. Elkus ; boards at European Hotel ;

King E. M., Coloma street ;

Kinney Richard, stable, Main st.; house, Center street ;

KIES GEO. O., publisher *El Dorado Times ;* boards at the Mountjoy House;

Kirk John, Superintendent of South Fork Canal Co.; house, west side Coloma street ;

KLINE M., confectionery and cigars, north side Main street, between Coloma street and the Plaza ;

Kohn Jacob, clerk with A. Bloch; house, n. s. Coloma st.;

Krauth Fred. K., printer ; house, Bedford avenue;

Kunkler Dr., physician, south side Main st., on the Plaza ;

Kunkler John E., south side Main street, on the Plaza;

Kunkle W., hostler, Redd's Stable, Main street.

L

Labeyrec Isidore, with Arvidsson & Co.; bds. at Lafayette ;
LACEY & HOGSETT, bakery and saloon, south side Main
    street, near Sacramento ;
Lacey William, of L. & H.; house, Sacramento street ;
Lampman J., teamster, east side Sacramento street ;
Lamb F. M., bricklayer, Cedar Ravine ;
LANDECKER LOUIS, groceries and provisions, cor. Main
    and Sacramento ; house, Main street, above Mill ;
Lang Adam, upholsterer, with Crisman ; h., Benham street ;
Landers C. S., boards at Cary House ;
LARGAN JAS. REV., pastor R. C. Church, Sacramento st.;
Lair Henry, butcher, with Conrad Etzel ;
Laundry City, Center street ;
Lavrien Lorenzo, clerk with G. Francis ; boards with same ;
Laury J., saloon, s. s. Main st., near Bedford Avenue ;
Lawrence John, miner, Cedar Ravine ;
Lawniker Louis, Main street ;
Lemon Samuel, of Freeman & Lemon ; Cedar Ravine Hotel ;
Leon G., packer ; house, near Bedford avenue ;
Leinorini Calvin, tailor, with Benjamin Wood ;
Leslie Andrew, miner, Log Cabin Ravine ;
Leslie Joseph, miner, Cedar Ravine ;
Levan D. W., Coloma street, east side ;
LEVISON MARK, clothing, north side Main street, near the
    Court House ; house, Main street ;
LOUIS & CO. H., dry goods, clothing and fancy goods, north
    side Main street, on the Plaza ;
Lewis H., of H. Louis & Co.;
Lewen Alfred, cook at National Restaurant ;
Livingston Max, clerk with Wolf ; boards at Cary House ;

ROBERT WHITE,
CHEMIST,
WHOLESALE AND RETAIL DRUGGIST,

Medical Hall, South Side Main Street, near Sacramento, Placerville,
and South Side Main Street, Upper Placerville.

Camphene, Alcohol, Kerosene and Lamp Oil, Paints,
Oils, Dye Stuffs, Lamp Chimneys,
Fancy Articles, etc., etc.

SCOVILL'S
SARSAPARILLA AND STILLINGIA!
Or, BLOOD AND LIVER SYRUP.

It is highly recommended by Physicians to cure the following diseases, having their origin in a disordered state of the blood : Scrofula, Tetter or Salt Rheum, Scald Head, Canker, Ulcerations and Enlargement of the Joints, Cancerous Tumors, Erysipelas, King's Evil, St. Anthony's Fire, White Swellings, Obstinate Eruptions, Pimples on the Face, Rheumatism, Blotches, Pustules, Dyspepsia, etc.; Syphilitic and Mercurial Affections are cured ; Chloresis or Obstructions in Females, Lucorrhœa or Whites, are relieved by this medicine.

The medical properties of Sarsaparilla in conjunction with Stillingia, are well known by all medical men to be the best compound yet discovered to cleanse and purify the blood, and eradicate all humors from the system. We have given the recipe to most Physicians in the country, that they may know what they are using ; and will continue to send it by mail to those desirous of knowing the ingredients entering into its composition, that they may prescribe it in their practice.

Thousands who have used the Stillingia and Sarsaparilla will testify to its remarkable effect in removing all impurities from their blood, giving tone and vigor to the whole human frame, and restoring a healthy action to all the functions of the body. As a Spring remedy, to purify and cleanse the blood, leaving it free from all humors and impurities, we assert, with confidence, there is no better remedy. Sold by all Druggists, and by

REDINGTON & CO., Agents, 409 and 411 Clay st., San Francisco,
To whom all orders should be addressed.

Logan O. B., tinsmith, Washington street;
Loney George, speculator, D. W. Levan's saloon;
Long John, laborer; boards at Orleans Hotel;
Long Adam, upholsterer, Main street; house, Benham st.;
Long Samuel, bricklayer; boards with J. Shira;
Looman J., toll-man; boards with Mrs. Bruce;
Lowell W. H., steward at Cary House;
Lundsberger A., clothing. n. s. Main st., on the Plaza;
LUNDBORG J. A. W., surgeon dentist, north west corner
    Main and Coloma streets, up stairs;
Lynch Patrick, of Hunter & Lynch;
Lynch Mat., miner; boards at New York House.

M

Mahon Mary, chambermaid at Cary House;
Mahoney John, saloon, head of Main street;
Malcom W. R., miner, Cedar Ravine;
Maloney Martin, blacksmith, at Alverson's;
Manning R., proprietor Mountjoy House;
Mannelle E., saloon, s. s. Main st., bet. Plaza and Bedford av.;
MARPLE W. L., paints, oils, glass, etc., north side Main
    street, near the Mountjoy House;
Matheney William, deputy collector; h., s. s. Washington st.;
Maynente L., Center street;
Maze & Co., Bella Union Saloon, Main street,
McBrien & Vanderbilt, saloon, n. s. Main st.;
BcBrien William, of McB. & V.; boards at Cary House;
McBride R. B., of Burns & McBride; boards at Cary House;
McCallum J. G.. attorney, City Block; h., e s. Bedford av.;
McCallum Geo., printer, *News* office; bds. with J. G. McC.
McCarthy M.. wheelwright, at Alverson's;
McClure J. E., wheelwright, for P. S. Co.;

McClure J. C., clerk at Cary House;

McCormick William, cook, at Cary House;

McCormick M. V. B., confectionery, north side Main street, between the Plaza and Bedford avenue;

McCone John, of Mead, Tasker & Co.; house, Coloma street, corner of Spring street;

McCusker Michael, miner; house, Mill street;

McDonald B., miner, Cedar Ravine;

McDonald C. B., Editor *Daily News ;*

McDougald J. A., city marshal; house, Chamberlain street;

McGinnis R. S., tinner; house, Main street;

McGinan R., miner, Cedar Ravine;

McGuch W., carpenter, Center street;

McIntire R. G., of Shearer & McIntire; bds. at Mountjoy;

McKinley J., lumber dealer, w. s. Main st.; bds. at Orleans;

McKean William, miner, Cedar Ravine;

McMahon Patrick, with W. M. Donahue; h., e. s. Coloma st.;

McMonagle Rev. J. H., Pastor Presbyterian Church; house, Coloma street;

McNeil Augustus, barber, with S. W. Huff;

Mead J. F., of Mead, Tasker & Co.;

Mead, Tasker & Co., Placerville Iron Works;

Meadows William, house painter, e. s. Sacramento street;

Medley P., blacksmith; boards Cedar street;

Mehany William, cook, at Cary House;

Meredith Charles, lawyer, corner Main and Coloma streets;

Mell Phœbe, hotel, Coloma street, near Main;

Melvin A. T., Gas Works; house, Coloma street;

Methven D. C., painter, east side Sacramento street;

Metzler M. S., of J. White & Co.; boards at Cary House;

Metzler John, clerk, at Mountjoy House;

Metropolitan Bath House, s. s. Main st., bet. Coloma and Plaza;

Meyer G., north side Main street;

MICHAELS V., Daguerreian Artist, north side Main street between Coloma and Plaza; boards at Mountjoy House;

Mierson & Jewell, clothing, s. s. Main street, on the Plaza;

Mierson Samuel, of Mierson & Jewell;

Milge & Co., Hope and Neptune Restaurant;

Milge Peter, of Milge & Co.;

Miller John, Proprietor National Restaurant;

Miller John, pastry cook, at Cary House;

Misch & Co., saloon, south side Main street, on the Plaza;

Misch Louis, of Misch & Co.;

Mitchner John, clerk, at Mountjoy House;

Moch J. A., of S. Haas & Co.; h., s. s. Main st., above Mill;

Molbus F., shoemaker, Main street; house, Benham street;

Mona A. milkman, Cedar Ravine;

Montini L., waiter at Lafayette Restaurant;

Montgomery Wm., gardener, Cottage st., next to Synagogue;

Moody William, cook, at Orleans Hotel;

Moody S., cook, at Orleans Hotel;

Morris P., waiter at Adriatic Restaurant;

Morris William, teamster, east side Bedford avenue;

MORRILL G. P., druggist, north side Main street, on the Plaza; house, south side Washington street;

Morrow John B., tinsmith; boards at Orleans Hotel;

Morrow James C., tailor, with J. M. Stewart;

Morrow James, barkeeper, with Weymouth & Clees;

Morena P., packer, Chapel street;

Moyhattu Charles, laborer; boards at Orleans Hotel;

MOUNTJOY HOUSE, north side Main st., near Stony Point;

Mountjoy G. N., clerk, with Hernandez & Anderson;

Mountjoy C. W., boards at Mountjoy House;

Munson Bros., meat market, south side Main street, between the Plaza and Bedford avenue;

Munson D. L., of Munson Bros.;

Munson J. R., of Munson Bros.;

Munson J., of Munson Bros.;

Murphy C. T., clothing, north side Main street, between the Plaza and Bedford avenue;

Murphy S., Esmeralda House, Main st., near Cedar Ravine;

Murphy Sarah, dress maker, Main st., opposite Cedar Ravine;

Murphy Agnes, dress maker, Main st., opposite Cedar Ravine;

Murtagh C., wheelwright; boards at Esmeralda House;

Murray B. F., carpenter, Spring street;

Murray ——, butcher, Main street; house, Mill street;

Murray Johanna, washing, Sacramento street;

Murgotten Henry, carpenter, Bedford avenue.

N

Nachman A., hardware, north side Main street, near Coloma; house, New Road;

Nand J., restaurant, Sacramento street;

Nary Mary, laundress, Cary House;

NASH I. H., hardware and stoves, north side Main street, opposite the Theater; house, e. s. Bedford avenue;

Nash H., house, Chapel street;

NATIONAL RESTAURANT, s. s. Main st., near Coloma;

Nelligan William, bootmaker, with Geo. Bottger;

Newbauer D., house, east side Coloma street;

New York House, C. Hilbert, proprietor, Main street;

Noe David, carpenter, Center street;

Noel William, carpenter; boards at Cedar Ravine Hotel;

Nolen W., steward at Mountjoy House;

Nolton William, speculator; with Hunter & Lynch;

Norris William, driver for P. S. Co.; boards at Cary House;

NUGENT THOMAS C., books, etc., north side Main street, between Coloma and Plaza; boards at Cary House.

O

Oasis Saloon, s. s. Main street, between Coloma and Plaza;
O'Brien Michael, laborer; west side Coloma street;
O'Donnell John, Theater Saloon, s. s. Main st., on the Plaza;
Odd Fellows' Hall, n. s. Main st., bet. Plaza and Bedford av.;
Ollis H., blacksmith, Main street;
ORT AUGUSTE, Lafayette Restaurant, n. s. Main street,
    between Coloma and the Plaza;
OWENS & Co., proprietors Empire Bakery, s. s. Main street,
    on the Plaza;
Owens D., of D. Owens & Co.

P

Packard W. P., clerk, Orleans Hotel;
PACKER J. J., painter, Main street, near Cedar Ravine;
Padducks William, hostler, Canal street.
Palmer George S., of Carr & Palmer; boards Mountjoy House;
Patten James, Cary alley;
Patten Thomas B., County Clerk, boards at Cary House;
Peacock John, miner; boards at Alderson's;
Pearson John, liquors, Main street, house Cedar Ravine;
Pearson Charles, tinner with Hanak & Sesser;
Pearson Alex., house, Pacific street;
PEBELIE & Co., J. A., Bath House and Barber Shop,
    Cary House.
Pebelie J. A., of J. A. Pebelie & Co., house, Mill street;
Pedlar Elijah, miner, boards at Alderson's Exchange;
PERKINS JACOB L., County Treasurer, Court House;
PHIPPS JAS., harnessmaker, Sacramento street, near Main;
Philbrick Wm., tinner, with I. H. Nash, boards at Mountjoy;

Phillip Louis, tailor, s. s. Main street, bet. the Plaza and
    Bedford avenue ;
Pinkham J. F., news agent, *News* office, house n. s. Main st.;
Pinney Albert, laborer, Benham street ;
Pioneer Stage Co., office, Cary House ;
Pitarein Maria, washing, Cedar Ravine :
PLANT H. T., proprietor Orleans Hotel ;
Platt J., stone mason, Cedar Ravine ;
Platt F. C., clerk with Burns & McBride ;
Platt C. W., jailor, Court House ; house, Cottage street ;
Post P., carpenter, house Washington street ;
PORTER J. S., Dr. (colored) physician ;
Price Maria, washing, north side Main street ;
Profferty Jacob, barber with J. Vantine ;
Pullen J. N., carpenter ; boards Cedar Ravine Hotel ;
Putnam A., driver P. S. Co.; boards Cary House.

Q

Query Douglas, miner, Cedar Ravine ;
Quixley Thos., boards New York House, Main street.

R

Radjesky Henry, cigar stand, Cary House ;
Radignet Anne, saloon, s. s. Main street, near Saramento ;
Randall George, shoemaker, Main street; h., Cedar Ravine ;
Ran Adolph, stone cutter ; boards Globe Hotel ;
Rankin A., west side Bedford avenue ;
RANKIN B. P., attorney, s. s Main, opp. Coloma st.;
    house, Sacramento street ;
Raphael H. T., clerk with A Kahn, boards with same ;
Raphan John, teamster; boards with Mahony ;
Raymond A., packer ; boards at Cary House ;

Ray Nelson, miner, house, Sacramento street;

Redlish S., clerk with H. Lewis & Co.;

Redd Robert, stable keeper; boards at Cedar Ravine Hotel;

Reddy Thomas, at Placerville Brewery;

Redd R. H., livery stable, Main st.; bds. Cedar Ravine Hotel;

Refagie B., north side Main street, on the Plaza;

Rehl Henry, clerk with L. Landecker;

Reilly Mary, milliner with Mrs. Irwin, house s. s. Coloma st.;

Rendle G. A. F., shomaker, n. s. Main st., above the Plaza;

Renand Pierre, gardener, Chamberlain street;

Res Charles, El Dorado Saloon, n. s. Main st., near Coloma;

Reynolds ——, teamster, Cedar Ravine;

Reynolds James M., treasurer of S. F. Canal Co., house west
side Sacramento street;

Reynolds J. J., policeman, house, Pacific street;

Rhodes A. J., at Tatterstalls stables; bds. at Orleans Hotel;

Richardson J. O., clerk with Bye & Stewart, h. Chamberlain st.;

Richardson L. B. & Co., groceries, s. s. Main st., opp. Coloma;

Richardson L. B., of L. B. Richardson & Co.;

Riley Francis, house, Center street;

Robinson J. B., bootmaker with F. Brasee; bds. at Mountjoy;

Roberts Samuel, farmer and blacksmith, C. V. road, house
west side of Bedford avenue;

Roberts F. M., speculator, Oasis Saloon, house, e. s. Coloma st.;

Robson P., speculator, Oasis Saloon, house e. s. Coloma st.,

Rockwell Peter, house, Chamberlain street.;

Rochots Morris, clerk with S. Haas & Co., bds. J. A. Mock;

Roff H. L., clerk with Wells, Fargo & Co.,

Rogers W. H. postmaster, house w. s. Clay street;

Rogers George, hostler, boards at Orleans Hotel;

Roman Simon; clerk with Mark Levison;

Romo Rafael, saloon, n. s. Main street, above the Plaza;

Ronda Andrew, teamster, boards at Alderson's Exchange;

Rosetta Alex., waiter, Hope and Neptune Restuarant;

Rose F., butcher with Armstrong & Hunger ;

ROY JOHN, furniture, Coloma street, house, Spring street;

Royce H. C., printer, *Republican* office ; bds. at Orleans Hotel ;

Russell C., harness maker with A. A. Van Voorhies ;

Russell J. B., of Brusce & Russell ; boards at Mountjoy;

Ryan Thomas, laborer, house, Spring street;

Ryan John, laborer, house, Spring street.

S

Sackrider Charles, driver for P. S. Co.; boards at Cary House ;

Sanborn J. H., clerk, with Hunt & Chace; bds. at Mountjoy ;

Sanderson S. W., attorney, next to Cary House, up stairs;
house, west side Coloma street;

Saulsbury M. J., clerk, with Hanak & Sesser; bds. Orleans ;

Sawyer George, speculator, Oasis Saloon ; h,, e. s. Coloma st.;

Schwartz ——, Benham street ;

SCHULTZ GEORGE, bakery, south side Main street, between the Plaza and Stony Point ;

Schnabs J. K., miner, Cedar Ravine ;

Schley Philip, cook, at Adriatic Restaurant ;

Schroder F., baker, with Sieg, Coloma street, near Main ;

Schomp J., teamster, Mill street ;

Scranton E., boards at Orleans Hotel ;

SEARLE A. C., Notary, next to Cary House, up stairs; bds.
at Orleans Hotel ;

Sealey William, house, Sacramento street ;

SEELEY J. W., watchmaker and jeweler, south side Main
street, near the Theater ; boards at Cary House ;

Sesser J. S., of Hanak & Sesser; boards at Cary House ;

Shaw Geo., telegraph operator, California State Telegraph Co.;

Shattuck C. W., teamster, west side Bedford avenue ;

Shepherd J. A., blacksmith ; boards at Cedar Ravine Hotel ;

J. H. WILLIAMS,..THOS. B. WADE.

J. H. WILLIAMS & CO.,

Wholesale and Retail Dealers in

WINES, LIQUORS AND CIGARS,

North side Main street, between Coloma street and the Plaza,

PLACERVILLE.

NATIONAL RESTAURANT,

South side Main street, between Coloma street and the Plaza,

PLACERVILLE.

MILGE & CO.,..........................PROPRIETORS.

☞ Oysters, Game, and all the Delicacies of the Season, constantly on hand. ☞ Go there, if you want a good *square* meal.

OASIS SALOON,

D. D. JOHNS..................PROPRIETOR,

South side Main st., between Coloma street and the Plaza,

PLACERVILLE.

———

THE CHOICEST BRANDS OF LIQUORS AND CIGARS.

JAS. L. WEYMOUTH,.....................................J. P. CLEES.

KNICKERBOCKER SALOON,

WEYMOUTH & CLEES,............. PROPRIETORS,

South side Main street, opposite Coloma street,

PLACERVILLE.

Shira J., miner, north side Main street ;

SHEARER & McINTIRE, attorneys, north side Main st.,
between the Plaza and Bedford avenue;

Shearer M. K., of Shearer & McIntire ;

Sheilds J. W., house, east side Coloma street ;

Sicandi John, teamster, County Road ;

Sickles John, driver P. S. Co.; boards at Cary House ;

SILBERMANN & CO. P., clothing, Old Round Tent, on the
Plaza ;

Silbermann P., of P. S. & Co.; boards at Orleans Hotel ;

SILBERSTEIN S., cigars, toys, etc., north west corner Main
and Coloma streets ;

Sieg F., bakery and saloon, Coloma street, corner Center ;

Siqueiras Joaquin, packer, Chapel street ;

Sims Claus, waiter, at Placer Hotel ;

Simms Henry, house, Cedar Ravine ;

Sinn R., cook, at Orleans Hotel ;

Sing Ye, washing, n. s. Main st., bet. Plaza and Bedford av.;

Sing Lin, supply store, Sacramento street ;

Sinnett F., moulder ; boards at Orleans Hotel ;

Skerrett E. E., Coloma street ;

Slavin John, laborer ; boards at Esmeralda House ;

Slevean Patrick, of Owens & Co.;

Sloss Henry C., of Hume & Sloss ; boards at Cary House ;

Sons Jacob, waiter, at Placer Hotel ;

SOUTH FORK CANAL COMPANY, office, south side
Main street, next to Cary House, up stairs ;

Smart K., carpenter, Mill street ;

Smith J. W., barkeeper, with Lew. Keller ;

Smith & Furness, saloon, s. s. Main st., bet. Coloma and Plaza ;

Smith Thomas, of Smith & Furness ;

Smith Mary A., north side Main street, near Cedar Ravine ;

Smith J. A., miner ; house, Main street ;

Smith J. J., laborer; boards at Orleans Hotel;
Smyth W. M., miner; house, east side Sacramento street;
SPRAGUE O. A., stage agent; boards at Orleans Hotel;
Squires Ogden, deputy Co. Clerk; house, east side Bedford av.;
Stark Jacob, wheelwright, with Orris, Main street;
STEINBERG M., pawnbroker, north side Main street, between Coloma and Plaza; house, Quartz alley;
Stephens N., steward, at Mountjoy House;
Stevens J. N., boards at Cedar Ravine Hotel;
Stevens James, stone-mason; boards with S. Murphy;
Stevens John, teamster; house, Cedar Ravine;
Stewart W. M., of Bye & Stewart; house, Coloma street;
STEWART J. M., merchant tailor, north side Main street, between the Plaza and Bedford avenue;
St. Louis House, north side Main street, near Bedford avenue;
Stipp H. S., printer; house, west side Bedford avenue;
Stone H. E., clerk; boards with J. Shira;
STORY D. W. C., water agent, District 9, South Fork Canal; house, Coon Hill;
Strauss David, Jr., clerk, with S. Bamberger;
Stroud J. R., clerk, with R. J. VanVoorhies & Co.;
Sturtevant William, carpenter, Center street;
Sullivan J., at Rev. J. Largan's, Sacramento street;
Supp Christian, of Wunsch & Supp, Placer Hotel;
SYMONS HENRY, Arcade Restaurant, north side Main st., between Plaza and Coloma street; house, Cedar Ravine;

T

Tasker Charles, of Mead, Tasker & Co.
Taylor O. Jr., carpenter, Mill street; house, Canal street;
Taylor David, driver P. S. Co.; boards at Cary House;
Thompson Mrs. N., boards with Mrs. Cole, Bedford avenue;
Thal H. H., vegetables, s. s. Main st., above the Plaza;

Thackham John, painter, east side Sacramento street;

Thatcher Wm., livery stable, Sacramento st.; bds. at Orleans;

Thatcher Jacob, livery stable, Sacramento st.; bds. at Orleans;

Tillman R. R., laborer, Sacramento street;

Titus I. S., of Cooke & Titus; house, High street;

Ti John, medicines, Sacramento street;

Tona J., miner; boards at Orleans Hotel;

Tolo Y., packer; house, Chapel street;

Townsend C., cabinet maker, Coloma near Main street;

TRACY T. F., agent for Wells, Fargo & Co., and P. S. Co.,
    house, west side Coloma street;

Tracy H. N., bootmaker with F. Brasee; bds. at Mountjoy;

Trempe John, El Dorado Saloon, n. s. Main street;

Tripp H., miner, Cedar Ravine;

Trumble M. E., book-keeper; boards at Orleans Hotel;

Tucker George, butcher; boards at Mountjoy House;

Tucker D. W., butcher with Munson & Bros.;

Turner C. B., bakery, Main street; house, Pacific street;

Turner John, teamster, Cedar Ravine;

Turk B., laborer, west side Sacramento street;

Turman H. B., blacksmith; boards at Mountjoy House.

V

Vance George, teamster, Main street;

Vance James; teamster, Main street;

Vanderbilt J. H., of McBrien & Vanderbilt; house east
    side of Coloma street;

VANGEISTEFIELD LOUIS, barber, s. s. Main st., bet.
    Coloma and the Plaza, house, Center street;

VANTINE JOHN, Oasis Bathing Saloon, s. s. Main st.,
    between Coloma and the Plaza;

Vaughn E. P., carpenter, Bedford avenue;

Van Eaton John, policeman; house, Washington street;

VAN VOORHIES A. A. saddlery and harness, s. s. Main
    street, between Coloma and Plaza; house w. s. Coloma st;
Van Voorhies Henry, with A. A. Van Voorhies;
VAN VOORHIES & Co., R. J. druggists, s. s. Main street,
    between Coloma and the Plaza;
Van Voorhies R. J., of R. J. V. V. & Co.; boards Cary House;
Vedder Abraham, carpenter, Main street;
Vedder Tacarius, tailor with B. Wood;
Vidal Salinas, jeweler, n. s. Main street above the Plaza;
Vonmeth Charles, laborer ; boards Reservoir street.

W

Wade Thomas B., of J. H. Williams & Co.; h. e. s. Coloma st.;
Wagner John, barkeeper with Sieg, Coloma street;
Wagget Catharine, washing, Benham street;
Wah Cum, tailor, Sacramento street;
WALKER & FLANAGAN, wholesale liquor dealers, north
    side Main street, on the Plaza;
Walker David, of Walker & Flanagan;
Wallace S. B., clerk; house, High street;
Walters Daniel, with B. Wood;
Warner W., of Misch & Co.;
Watson Henry, hostler; boards at Orleans Hotel;
Watson Charles, driver P. S. Co.; boards at Cary House;
Weiner C., clerk with S. Harris;
Welch George, with S. Murphy, Main street;
Welton E. W., surveyor, City Block, Main street;
Wells, Fargo & Co., office Cary House building;
Westlake H., packer; boards at Cary House;
Wetherell William, Le Roy street;
WEYMOUTH & CLEES, saloon, s. s. Main st., opp. Coloma;
Weymouth J. L., of Weymouth & Clees; bds. Cary House;
Whelan Kate, teacher ; boards with McCone, w. s. Coloma st.;

WHITE & Co., JOSEPH, bankers, Cary House building ;

White J., of J. White & Co.; house, e. s. Coloma street ;

White D. J., clerk with W. F. & Co.; boards at Cary House ;

WHITE ROBERT, druggist, s. s. Main st., near Sacramento ;
boards at Cary House ;

Wickham H., miner ; boards at Orleans Hotel ;

Wier W., vegetables, s. s. Main st., bet. Coloma and Plaza ;

WILLETS S., County Recorder ; boards at Cary House ;

Williamson J. H., clerk with L. Landecker ; bds. at Orleans ;

WILLIAMS & Co., J. H., wholesale and retail liquors, north
side Main street, bet. Coloma and Plaza ;

Williams J. H., of J. H. W. & Co.; h. e. s. Sacramento st.;

Williams J. J., of Eastman & Williams attorneys ;

Williams David, carpenter,

Wilson F. L., miner ; boards with E. L. Kinney ;

Wisty Jacob, grocer, Main street ;

Wong Ah, washing, north side Main street ;

WOLF BROS., dry goods, s. s. Main st., between the Plaza
and Coloma street ;

Wolf Ludwig, of Wolf Brothers ;

Wolf Henry, of Wolf Brothers ;

W olinich M., waiter at National Restaurant ;

WOOD BENJAMIN, tailor, s. s. Main street, on the Plaza ;

Woodworth E. west side Sacramento street ;

Wonderlin S., clerk with W. M. Donahue ; bds. Placer Hotel ;

Wright H. A. carpenter ; house, Pacific street ;

Wright W. V,, carpenter ; house, Pacific street ;

WUNSCH & SUPP, proprietors Placer Hotel, n. s. Main
street, between Coloma st., and the Plaza ;

Wunsch Henry, of Wunsch & Supp.

Y

Yarnell & Co., George, of *Daily News*, n. s. Main street,
   bet. Coloma street, ard the Plaza ;
Yarnell George, of George Yarnell & Co.; bds. with Mrs. Cole ;
Young John, hostler ; boards at Orleans Hotel.

Z

Zeigler J. B., European Hotel, n. s. Main st., near Coloma ;
Zigler ——, teacher, Cedar Ravine.

PLACERVILLE REPUBLICAN
NEWSPAPER,
Book and Job Printing
ESTABLISHMENT.

—

THOMAS FITCH & CO.
PROPRIETORS.

—

(OFFICE, IN SEBASTOPOL HALL.)

—

"NEAT, CHEAP AND RAPID!"
IS OUR MOTTO.

—

Terms of the Placerville Republican:

Single copy, one year.................................$5 00
Single copy, six months............................. 3 00
Single copy, three months.......................... 1 50
Single copy, one month............................. 50

INVARIABLY IN ADVANCE,

AGENTS OF THE REPUBLICAN.

C. A. CRANE, Northwest corner Washington and Sansome streets, Government Building, up stairs, San Francisco.

H. S. HULBURD is authorized to solicit subscriptions, advertisements, etc.

D. C. HUMPHREYS is authorized to act as our Traveling Agent, to receive subscriptions, advertisements, etc.

HENRY JACOBS is our authorized Agent for Georgetown.

JOHN FOX is our Agent at Carson City, and will attend to all business for us faithfully and promptly.

PART II.
—
UPPER PLACERVILLE.

UPPER PLACERVILLE DIRECTORY.

A.

Allen Thomas, wood dealer, north side Main street;
Anstee Henry, miner, south side Main street ;
Anderson J. M., south side Main street;
American House, south side Main street.

B

Berry John M., livery and feed stable, s. s. Broadway street ;
Bliss George F., miner; boards Nevada House ;
BOWMAN C. J. proprietor Union House ;
Bradshaw & Co., books and stationery, n. s. Market street ;
Bradshaw William, of B. & Co.; boards Nevada House ;
Branch of Medical Hall, drugs and medicines, Broadway st.;
BREWSTER & Co. C. W., bankers and merchants, n. e.
    cor. Washington and Broadway streets ;
Brewster C. W., of B. & Co.; house, e. s. Washington st ;
Brewster J., of B. & Co.; house, e. s. Washington street;
Brooks L., miner ; boards Nevada House ;
Bronson James, farmer, south side Broadway street ;
Bronson Russell, farmer south side Broadway street ;
Brown T., miner ; boards at Nevada House ;
Brown J. H., miner ; boards at Nevada House ;
Brown S. A., book-keeper with T. Wilcox ;
Brown Gustavus, tailor with C. W. Brewster & Co.,
BURTON L. J. & McK., proprietors Nevada House ;
Burns J, P., farmer, north side Main street;
Burnham George, of Howlett & Burnham, s. s. Main st.

C

California Brewery, south side Main street ;
Cannavan P., shoemaker, south side Broadway street ;
Campbell Peter, blacksmith, with Wonderly ;
Carpenter J. D., livery and feed stable, east end Main street ;
Church S. M., teamster ; boards at Nevada House ;
Christian William, baker, west side Bridge street ;
Cody T. T., stock raising, south side Washington street ;
Cody P. H., dairy, south side Washington street ;
Coleman James, blacksmith with Spencer & Ludinghouse ;
Collins H. M., clerk with T. Wilcox ;
Compton L. F., carpenter ; boards at Nevada House ;
Corwing B. W., tinsmith ; boards at Nevada House ;
Crocker W. H., farmer, south side Washington street ;
Crocker Benjamin, hay yard, south side Washington street ;
Culver R, P., lumber dealer, north side Broadway street ;
Culver Lewis, clerk with R. P. Culver.

D

Davis Daniel, wagon maker, north side Broadway street ;
Ditson William, farmer, north side Washington street ;
Dooris Mrs. fruit dealer, south side Main street.

E

El Dorado House, corner Main and Bridge streets ;
Englesfried Jacob. south side Main street ;
Ewell John, miner, west side Washington street.

F

Fisher L. P. school teacher ; boards at P. P. Hoxie's ;
Flagg N., merchant, cor. Main & Bridge street ;
Foster J. W., farmer, north side Broadway street ;
Foster J. H., farmer, north side Broadway street.

G

Gates Franklin, assayer with C. W. Brewster & Co.;
Garrett J. R., druggist, Medical Hall ;
Gilda Charles, tailor with Sill & Meacham ;
Gillett Edson, south side Main street.

H

Hartwell C. N., of S. N. Woods & Co. merchants ;
Henderson William, engineer, south side Main street ;
Hermance W. P., packer ; boards at Nevada Hotel;
House William, miner, west side Broadway street :
HOWLETT & BURNHAM, merchants, cor. Bridge and
    Market streets ;
Howlett George W., of H. & B.; boards at Nevada House ;
Hoxie P. P., miner, north side Broadway street ;
HUFF JOHN, barber, south side Main street ;
Hulburd H. S., general agent, north side Broadway street ;
Huntington J. C., miner, south side Main street ;
Huntington Wilber, miner, south side Main street ;
Hunsberger Levi, farmer, north side Broadway street.

J

Johnson Walter, miner, south side Washington street ;
Johnson John, miner, north side Broadway street.

T. WILCOX,

WHOLESALE DEALER IN

PROVISIONS, FLOUR, GRAIN,

FEED, LIQUORS, GROCERIES, ETC.,

MARKET STREET, UPPER PLACERVILLE.

CHARLES H. LEIFRIED,

HARNESS - MAKER AND CARRIAGE - TRIMMER,

OPPOSITE C. W. BREWSTER & CO.'S,

UPPER PLACERVILLE.

WILLIAM SIGMUND,

MEAT MARKET,
Upper Placerville.

Will at all times keep on hand an assortment of the finest quality of MEATS of all kinds.

S. N. WOODS & CO.,

Wholesale and Retail Dealers in

GROCERIES, PROVISIONS, WINES, LIQUORS,

Also, WINDOWS AND DOORS,

UPPER PLACERVILLE.

S. N. WOODS,............................C. N. HARTWELLL.

K

Kelly E., teamster ;
Kossman Edward, proprietor Washington House ;
KUHN F. W., physician and surgeon, w. s. Washington st.

L

Lambert H., clerk with Woods & Co.;
Larned W., miner ; boards at Nevada House ;
Leifried C. A., harness maker, south side Broadway street ;
Lockard J. M., teamster ;
Ludinghouse F., of Spencer & Lundinghouse, west side
    Washington street;
Lyons William, farmer, south side Washington street.

M

Macomber Philander, miner, south side Broadway street ;
Martin S., miner, east side Washington street;
Masonic Hall, south side Broadway street ;
McCall John, farmer, north side Washington street ;
McCall James, farmer, north side Washington street ;
McCormick William, dairy, south side Washington street ;
McGinnis Samuel, miner, south side Broadway street;
McKinly & Co., lumber dealers, north side Main street ;
Meacham B., of Sill & Meacham, n. s. Broadway street;
Meadows William, painter, south side Broadway street;
Middleton J. T., shoemaker, south side Broadway street ;
Miller W. N., livery stable, north side Main street;
Miller John, miner ;
Moore Franklin, teamster, south side Washington street ;
Morphy William, clerk with Howlett & Burnham;
Myers Mathew, cooper, south side Main street.

NEVADA HOTEL,

BROADWAY, UPPER PLACERVILLE.

McK. & L. J. BURTON,............................ PROPRIETORS.

☞ Superior Accommodations for Families.   Stage Office for Sacramento and other places.

J. SUMNER, Agent,

Wholesale and Retail Dealer in

STOVES, TIN-WARE, HARD-WARE,

Iron and Steel, Blacksmith and Carpenter's Tools, Tom Iron, Lead Pipe, Pumps, Copper, Zinc and Tin Plate, Crockery and House-Furnishing Goods, etc.   All kinds of Copper, Tin and Sheet-Iron work made to order, at short notice.

Corner Washington and Broadway streets,

UPPER PLACERVILLE.

D. D. SILL,..*B. MEACHAM.*

SILL & MEACHAM,

Wholesale and Retail Dealers in

Staple and Fancy Dry Goods,

Blankets, Carpets, Clothing, Boots, Shoes, Hats, etc.

☞ Clothing made to order, and all kinds of Machine Sewing done with dispatch.

Fire-Proof Building, corner Washington and Market streets,

UPPER PLACERVILLE.

N

Nevada House, north side Broadway street.

O

Orn Joseph, packer with T. Wilcox.

P

Parlow N., miner, north side Broadway street ;
Parkhurst O., salesman with C. W. Brewster & Co.,
Persing W. G., miner ; boards at Nevada House ;
Pew B. F., farmer, south side Broadway street ;
Phelps W. W., printer ; house, s. s. Washington street ;
Potthoff William, proprietor El Dorado House.

R

Ranney George C., carpenter, south side Washington street ;
Ransom John, farmer, south side Washington street ;
Raymond A. C., agent for W. L. Perkins ;
Robertson John, farmer, south side of Washington street ;
Rolling Charles, brewer, California Brewery.

S

Scott John, carpenter, at McKinly & Co., n. s. Main street ;
Shoup S., hostler, at Carpenter's livery stable ;
SIGMUND W., meat market, north side Market street ;
SILL & MEACHAM, merchants, corner Market and Washington streets ;
Sill D. D., of S. & M.; boards at Nevada House ;
Simonton Adam, constable, west side Washington street ;
Sinclair Samuel F., merchant, south side Main street ;

CALIFORNIA BREWERY,

SOUTH SIDE MAIN STREET,

UPPER PLACERVILLE.

JACOB ZEISZ,.....................PROPRIETOR.

☞ The best quality of LAGER BEER always on hand.
Families and others supplied with any size package desired.

George W. Howlett,.................................... George Burnham.

HOWLETT & BURNHAM,

Wholesale and Retail Dealers in

Groceries, Liquors, Provisions,

Flour, Grain, California Produce, and General Merchandise,

Fire-Proof Building, corner Bridge and Market streets,

UPPER PLACERVILLE.

EVERY VARIETY OF

Book and Job Printing

Neatly, cheaply and expeditiously executed at the Office of

The Placerville Republican.

(OFFICE, IN SEBASTOPOL HALL.)

PLACERVILLE.

Smith W., hose maker, south side Main street;
Smith Mrs., laundress, south side Main street;
Smith H., teamster, Nevada House;
Smith E. H., teamster, south side Main street;
Smith Anthony, south side Main street;
Snider L., cook, Nevada House;
Spencer & Ludinghouse, blacksmiths and wagonmakers, west
      side Bridge street;
Spencer L., of S. & L., west side Bridge street;
Stone D., proprietor American House, south side Main street;
STOUT & BERRY, livery stable, west side Bridge street;
Stout T. B., of S. & B.; boards at Washington House;
STOUT G. W., Justice of the Peace, n. s. Broadway street;
Stowell George, teamster, north side Washington street;
Stowell Henry, laborer, south side Main street;
SUMNER J., agent, stoves, tin and hardware, cor. Washington
      and Broadway streets.

T

Taylor O. M., farmer, south side Broadway street;
Temperance Hall, south side Broadway street;
Thompson George, miner, south side Broadway street;
Tittler George, boards at Nevada House;
Turmin Byron, teamster, south side Broadway street.

U

Union House, corner Washington and Market streets.

V

Vosburg, I. N.; wagonmaker, south side Main street.

W

Washington House, north side Market street ;
Wheeler Rev. S. S., north side Broadway street ;
Wheeler R., livery stable, south side Broadway street ;
WILCOX T., merchant, south side Market street ;
Williamson J. Y., laborer, north side Broadway street ;
Woodward G. A., millwright ; boards at Nevada House ;
WOODS S. N. & Co., merchants, south side Broadway st.;
Woods S. N., of S. N. W. & Co.; house, s. s. Broadway st.;
Wonderly N., blacksmith and wagonmaker, n. s. Broadway st.;
Wright S., teamster, north side Broadway street.

Y

Young John, salesman with J. Sumner, agent.

Z

ZEISZ JACOB, proprietor California Brewery.

PART III.

EL DORADO.

HISTORY OF EL DORADO.

THE Town of El Dorado, formerly Old Mud Springs, was one of the first settled in the County, having been a mining camp as early as 1849–'50. It is situated on the public road leading from Placerville to Sacramento, about five miles westerly from the former city, and has at present a population of about twelve hundred. The old town took its name from springs (mud springs) near the present town. Like all other towns in mining districts, it owed its existence and growth to the rich mines in its vicinity, which consisted in extensive placers and a great number of gold-bearing quartz lodes, which have been generally worked since 1850–'51. Many ravines, gulches and creeks are tributary to the town, which have afforded ample pay for thousands of miners—principally, and among them, Empire Ravine, Dead Man's Hollow, Loafers' Hollow, Log Town Creek, Matheney's Creek, Slate and Dry Creeks.

One of the first settlers of the place was James Thomas, who, in the Winter of 1849–'50, erected, at what is now the upper portion of the town, a hotel and trading post, called the "Old Mud Springs House." As early as 1851 there were constructed upon or near Matheney's Creek, five steam quartz mills, at a cost of from $15,000 to $40,000 each. Four large mills were constructed on Logtown Creek the year following, and others in different directions in the vicinity ; taken together they have furnished employment for about five hundred laborers. Many of these mills have yielded to the pro-

prictors fabulous returns. The town, although located more
from accident than design, is situated in the midst of wide,
undulating valleys, of deep and productive vegetable mould,
already taken up and improved as farms, from which are produced yearly vast quantities of cereals, hay and stock; also
the soil and climate is particulary adapted to the growth of the
grape and orchards. It is also the junction of the Sacramento
and the road leading to Drytown, Jackson, Mokelumne Hill,
Stockton and Sonora—the survey of the great trunk railroad
stretching from San Francisco and Sacramento, *via* Placerville, to the Atlantic States, passes through the town—also a
turnpike road, upon a grade of not more than two and a-half
degrees, built at a cost of fifteen thousand dollars, now runs
between the town of El Dorado and Placerville. The number
of grape vines already planted in this vicinity, the most of
which are now bearing, amounts to about two hundred thous-
and, and the number of fruit trees to one hundred thousand.
There are twenty stone and brick fire-proof stores, some of
which, in costliness and elegance, are not surpassed by any in
the County. There is also a line of semi-daily stages running to Placerville, aside from the daily line running into this
place from Sacramento, Drytown, Jackson, etc., to Carson
Valley, and overland to St. Joseph.

The vineyards of Mr. W. H. Pavey and J. M. B. Wetherwax have this year produced hundreds of gallons of wine, of
the richest and most delicious aroma, and in body and quality
not surpassed by any foreign importation. G. G. Blanchard,
Esq., is cultivating a vineyard of about fifty acres, that, from
the quality of the vine, they being mostly of foreign varieties,
and the attention which the proprietor is bestowing upon it,
bids fair to be the finest vineyard in the County. The enter-
prise of the merchants has contributed much to the growth,

character and importance of the place. Messrs. Jackson, McCord and J. W. Jackson stand prominent amongst them. The St. Stephen's Parish of the Episcopal Church is located here—its Pastor, Mr. Pierce holds service twice a month. The Methodist Church also has services on each Sunday. There is also a school house, that in point of convenience, accommodation and costliness, is not excelled in the county, with a school inferior to none, and perhaps superior to any in the State. The Masons have a hall, two stories high, 30x50 feet, built of brick, nearly completed, the lower story is intended for a store and the upper part for a lodge hall. In the Winter of 1855 the Town was incorporated under its present name of El Dorado, by which it has been known ever since. There are three Attorneys, Geo. G. Blanchard, Chas. Meredith and Moses Tebbs; three Physicians, Dr. M. D. Hinman, Dr. L. Marotte and Dr. Bayliss. There is a branch of Wells, Fargo & Co.'s Express office, and a telegragh office, with James McCormick, Esq., agent and operator. The lumber yards of S. & J. Fleming & Co., and Rogers & Atwood add much to the business of the place. Messrs. Fleming making their yard a depot for the lumber of their two extensive saw mills above Pleasant Valley, on the Carson Valley road. El Dorado presents every appearance and possesses every element of permancy and importance, and will undoubtedly continue to grow and prosper with the rest of the County.

MASONS.

Hiram Lodge, No. 43, F. and A. M., commenced operations under a dispensation, October. 1853.

Charles Meredith ....Worthy Master
T. J. Orgon.................................Secretary

CHURCHES.

St. Stephen's Parish ; Pastor, Rev. C. C. Peirce.
Methodist Episcopal Church, South; Rev. Joseph Emery, Pastor.

OILS AND LAMPS.

STANFORD BROTHERS

Have in store a great variety of COAL OIL LAMPS, of every style of burner known to the trade.

Bracket Lamps and side Lamps, with the largest burners in use; Parlor and Stand Lamps—an endless variety of patterns; Chamber Lamps and Handle Lamps—very cheap, may be carried about; Chandeliers and Lanterns; Camphene Wicks; Chimneys, Shades, Globes, of every size, style and finish;

200 barrels Sperm Oil—at a lower price than ever before sold in this city; 100 barrels Lard Oil, of our own importation; 600 tubs Rape Seed Oil, in original packages; 100 barrels boiled Linseed Oil, guaranteed pure and free from fish oils; 400 cases Downer's Kerosene; 800 cases Coal Oils, at the very lowest market prices.

☞ We feel confident in assuring our customers and the trade generally, that they will find our assortment of Lamps and Lamp stock, as well as Oils and all kinds of Burning Materials, the most complete that has ever been offered on the Pacific Coast. Our purchases have been made upon the most advantageous terms, and we are determined to fix our prices at a standard so low that dealers in our line of goods can lay in their stocks, and have a wider margin for profit than they have ever had before. **STANFORD BROS.,**
121, 123, 125 California st., near Front, San Francisco.

S. AMBROSE'S

Ladies' and Gentlemen's Restaurant,

ICE CREAM SALOON AND FANCY BAKERY,

124 Montgomery street, between Bush and Sutter,

SAN FRANCISCO.

☞ Oysters, Game, Pies, Cakes, Confectionery, and all the Delicacies of the Season, constantly on hand. Families and Parties supplied at short notice.

EL DORADO DIRECTORY.

A

Allen Edwin, shoemaker, north side of Main street.
Atmore Richard (of Westcott & Atmore).
Atwood Alexander (of F. S. Rogers & Co.), s. s. South st.
Austin William, boards with H. D. Hinman.

B

Baldy John, clerk with C. P. Jackson & Co.
Black B. B., boards at Oriental Hotel.
Blackford S. M., boards at Nevada House.
Blanchard & Meredith, attorneys—office, south s. Main st.
Blanchard G. G., east side Placerville road.
Bayliss, M. D., William, boards at Roussin's.
Boswell Rufus, clerk at Fleming's.
Boyd Charles, proprietor Oriental Hotel.
Briggs Cyrus, teamster, south side Main street.
Burnham James, clerk with Price.
Butler John, teamster, south side South street.

C

Carmichael James, shoemaker, south side Main street.
Carpenter C., wagonmaker, north side Main street.
Cephas James (colored), barber, south side Main street.

Chambers Samuel, teamster.
Chambers D., miner.
Chavallier Andrew, miner.
Coombes Levi, miner, north side Main street.
Cooper David (colored), cook at Nevada Hotel.
Comins J., blacksmith, south side Main street.
Crane J. R., blacksmith, north side Main strcet.
Crane S. L., north side Main street.
Craven Joseph, mason, boards at Oriental Hotel.

D

Dakins William, teamster, south side South street.
Davis, L. M., farmer, south side Main street.
Davis, Bela F., teamster, south side Main street.
Davis J. R., boards at Lee's, north side Main street.
DEAN J. J., merchant—residence, north side North street.
DeWolfe J. B., saloon keeper, north side Main street.
Doneho Thomas, stage driver—residence, north side Main st.
Duckworth Edwin, miner, north side Main street.
Duckworth Robert, miner, north side Main street.

E

El Dorado, Diamond Springs and Placerville Stage Office—
    Nevada House, Main street.
Emery Joseph Rev., south side South street.

F

Falk Hiram, Justice of the Peace, south side Main street.
FITZGIBBON THOMAS, butcher, south side Main street.
Fleming A. C., clerk at Fleming & Co.'s.
FLEMING & CO., lumber dealers, south side Main street.
Floyd J., boot-black, north side Main street.

O. B. WESTCOTT, RICHARD ATMORE.

NEVADA HOUSE,

Corner of Main and Jackson Streets.

EL DORADO, CAL.

General Stage Office.

☞ This House is elegantly fitted up for the reception of Families and Travelers. Connected with the House is an extensive STABLE and CORRAL, with all the necessary accommodations.

WESTCOTT & ATMORE, Proprietors.

C. P. JACKSON, F. M. McCORD.

C. P. JACKSON & CO.,

Wholesale and Retail Dealers in

GROCERIES, PROVISIONS, GRAIN, GROUND FEED,

FRUIT, LIQUORS, CIGARS, ETC.,

El Dorado, California.

CHARLES P. JACKSON,

BANKER,

EL DORADO, CALIFORNIA.

☞ Checks on Sacramento and San Francisco. Exchange on Atlantic States and Europe.

G

GARDINER G. B., nurseryman, north side North street.
Golden J. M., clerk with H. D. Hinman.
Gunnison S., shoemaker, south side Main street.

H

Hathaway E., clerk with J. J. Dean.
Harwood Lyman, blacksmith, south side Main street.
Heninger T. J., carpenter, south side Main street.
Hinman H. D., physician and surgeon, north side Main st.
Houghton Mrs. Clarissa, south side South street.

I

Irwin J. W., miner, boards at Richwood House.

J

JACKSON C. P. & CO., merchants, south side Main street.
JACKSON C. P. (of Jackson & Co.), south side Main street.
Jackson J. L., bookkeeper at Jackson & Co,'s.
JACKSON J. W., merchant, north side Main street.
Johnson Nathan, boards at Oriental Hotel.

K

Kane James, clerk with T. Russell, south side Main street.
King M. D., saloon keeper, south side Main street.
Knapping Charles, steward Nevada House.
Kuchenmeister B., watchmaker, north side Main street.

L

Lasky M., merchant, north side Main street.
Lee John, ranchman, north side Main street.

MUD SPRINGS BREWERY,

Main Street,..........................**El Dorado.**

JOHN THIESEN, PROPRIETOR.

☞ None but the best materials used in manufacturing. LAGER BEER delivered free to all parts of the County. EL DORADO, January 1, 1862.

J. J. DEAN,

—— DEALER IN ——

Groceries, Provisions,

LIQUORS,

CROCKERY AND HARDWARE,

DRY GOODS, BOOTS, SHOES, ETC., ETC.,

Main street, one door above Wells, Fargo & Co.'s Office,

EL DORADO, CALIFORNIA.

GEORGE G. BLANCHARD,   CHARLES MEREDITH.

BLANCHARD & MEREDITH,

COUNSELORS AND ATTORNEYS-AT-LAW.

——

Offices at El Dorado and Placerville.

Levi Hyman, clerk, north side Main street.
Leiser Jacob, merchant, north side Main street.
Loose Frank, boards with J. Theisen.
Luttig Joseph, brewer, north side Main street.
Lumber Yard, F. S. Rogers & Co., south side South street.
Lumber Yard, Fleming & Co., south side Main street.

M

Maddox J. T., teamster, boards with T. Russell.
Matthews C. W., carpenter, south side North street.
Matthews Henry, mason, boards at Nevada House.
Marcas L., clerk with Laskey.
Marshall William, miner.
Martin Edward, butcher, south side Main street.
Marotte L., physician and surgeon, north side Main street.
Meredith Charles, lawyer—office, south side Main street.
McCarty Mrs. J., north side Main street.
McCORMICK JAMES, Wells, Fargo & Co.'s Agent, north
    side of Main street.
McCormick J. K., saloon keeper, south side Main street.
McCord F. M. (of C. P. Jackson & Co.), south side Main st.
Morrison Richard, north side Main street.
Morse Ira, carpenter, north side Main street.
Mud Springs Brewery, J. Theisen, proprietor, n. s. Main st.

N

NEVADA HOUSE, Westcott & Atmore, props., s. s. Main st.

O

Oreli Rocoi, painter, south side North street.
Organ Presley, miner, south side Main street.
ORGON THOMAS J., Notary Public, north side Main st.

Oriental Hotel, Charles Boyd, proprietor, north side Main st.

P

Pavey Charles, farmer, north side Main street.
Pavey W, H., Logtown street.
Penney R. M., farmer, with L. M. Davis.
Perry W. E., saloon keeper, north side Main street.
Potter I. H., boards at Oriental Hotel.
Price William, merchant, south side Main street.

R

Reynolds C. F., steward Oriental Hotel.
RHINE NATHAN, merchant, south side Main street.
Richwood House, Roussins, proprietors, south side South st.
ROGERS & CO., F. S., lumber dealers, south side South st.
Rogers F. S., surgeon dentist, south side South street.
Roussin Mrs. Ann, Richwood House.
Roussin C. P., Richwood House.
ROUSSIN C. T., Richwood House.
RUSSELL THOMAS, merchant, south side Main street.

S

Salmon Louis, clerk with Nathan Rhine.
Schlotyhaver Paul, baker, north side Main street.
SHERSEN JOHN, shoemaker, south side Main street.
SIMMONS J. E., constable, north side Main street.
Simmons Henry, north side Main street.
Smith & Co., livery stable, north side Main street.
Smith M. M., (of Smith & Co.)
Smith A. S., (of Smith & Co.)
Smith James, carriage maker, north side Main street.
Smith J. J., shoemaker, south side Main street.

STEERE ROBERT, postmaster, north side Main street.
Standeford D. W., ditch agent.
Standeford W. W., miner.
Stilwell S. M., butcher, south side Main street.
Strait B. B., teamster, boards at Nevada House.
Swandt R. W. H,, carpenter, boards at Roussin's.

T

Tebbs Moses, lawyer, office south side Main street.
Ten Eyck G. W., north side Main street.
THEISEN JOHN, brewer, residence north side North street.
THORNTON D., saddler, uorth side Main street.

W

Waidhaas Quirin, barber, north side Main street.
Wassam Jacob, farmer, north side Main street.
Wetherwax J. M. B., north side Main street.
Westcott O. B. (of Westcott & Atmore), Nevada House.
WILLOW E., farmer, north side Main street.
Woolover D., merchant, south side Main street.
WREHNAR ABA, merchant, north side Main street.

ABA WREHNAR,

—DEALER IN—

GROCERIES, PROVISIONS,

WINES, LIQUORS AND CIGARS,

HARD-WARE,

Grain and Ground Feed,

EL DORADO, CAL.

EVERY VARIETY OF

Book and Job Printing

Neatly, cheaply and expeditiously executed at the Office of

The Placerville Republican,

PLACERVILLE.

JAMES McCORMICK,

JUSTICE OF THE PEACE,

—AND—

AGENT FOR WELLS, FARGO & CO.,

MAIN STREET, EL DORADO.

☞ Deeds written and acknowledged.

PART IV.

—

GEORGETOWN.

CITIZENS'

Accommodation Stage Line.

PARKER & WELLINGTON........ PROPRIETORS.

FOLSOM AND GEORGETOWN,

—— AND ——

FOLSOM AND COLOMA.

George Gilbert, Agent,........ Sacramento and Folsom
H. Fuller, Agent,...........................Georgetown
J. W. Parker, Agent,........................Coloma

HENRY JACOBS,
(POSTMASTER,)
DEALER IN BOOKS AND STATIONERY,
CIGARS AND TOBACCO,

**Wall Paper, Window Shades, Cutlery, Silver-Plated Ware,
Fruit, Candies, etc.,**

Fire-Proof Brick,......................Georgetown.

Also, keeps constantly on hand a good stock of

Camphene, Kerosene, Coal Oil,

Lanterns, and General Varieties,

☞ **AT WHOLESALE AND RETAIL.** ☜

HISTORY OF GEORGETOWN.

THE TOWN OF GEORGETOWN is situated upon the beautiful high ground on the dividing ridge between the South and Middle Forks of the American River, about ten miles from the former and four miles from the latter. It was first settled in August, 1849, in a narrow ravine about one-eighth of a mile from its present location. In July, 1852, the whole of the business portion of the town was swept away by fire, after which event the town was rebuilt where it now stands. In July, 1856, another disastrous fire occurred, which destroyed most of the business houses, and many dwellings. Again, in 1858, a fire occurred, which swept off about one-half of the business places. Since that time no fires of any considerable importance have occurred.

This village has now a population of about 500, among whom are many families. Pretty cottages, surrounded with pleasant gardens, vines, fruit and shade trees, to be seen in every direction, give it a pleasant and prosperous appearance, convincing the most casual observer that its inhabitants have full confidence in its permanence. Of public buildings, it contains one Church, (Catholic,) one Theater, a School House, and Town Hall. The Methodist denomination hold service regularly, every Sabbath, in the Town Hall. The Catholics have service on the first Sabbath of each month. There is a District School taught regularly, with an attendance of from thirty to forty pupils. There are a large number of merchants, representing almost every department of trade, who seem to be doing well; one Banking House and Express Office, three

Hotels, two Livery and Sale Stables, Wagon and Blacksmith
Shops, one Harness and Saddlery Shop, one Steam Saw Mill,
and one Water Saw Mill, about two miles from the town.
From the first settlement of this place, it has been noted for
its rich mines. Many of the gulches about here have yielded
almost fabulous amounts to their fortunate workers. There
seems a greater degree of lasting permanence to the mines
about here than in most placer diggings, and they seem likely
to afford profitable employment for many years to the patient,
enterprising miner. The miners and agriculturalists are mostly
supplied with water from "The Pilot Creek Water Co.," an
incorporation: Trustees, E. H. Watson, W. H. Stone, D. C.
McKenney; President, D. C. McKenney; Secretary and
Treasurer, W. H. Stone; Superintendent, E. H. Watson.
The ditches of this company are about fifty miles in length,
and furnish water all the season, supplying miners as low
down as Kelsey and Wild Goose Flat, and intermediate places.

Agriculture, in the vicinity of Georgetown, has attained an
importance worthy of notice. "As late as 1856, the lands
about here were regarded as barren and worthless. The gold
mines and the timber were supposed to be all that was valuable. A few experiments, conducted on a limited scale, however, led to the belief that something might be done in regard
to agriculture. The small efforts at raising garden vegetables were in many cases successful, and the very few peach
and apple trees planted by the miners seemed to grow very
well. In 1857-'8 a number of small orchards in the vicinity
of the town, and an extensive nursery, were started. These
have all done remarkably well, and the disposition to plant
fruit trees has become very general. The red land of this
district seems adapted, in a pre-eminent degree, to the growth
of the apple and the grape, while the peach tree is less vigor-
ous and productive than upon lower and richer lands. As w

ascend the sides of the mountain there is a general improve-
ment in the quality of all fruits, so far up as the trees grow
vigorously, and the fruit has time to ripen. Here, at an ele-
vation of 2,500 feet above tide-water, the best varieties of the
apple of New England, New York, and the North-western
States come to great perfection, and will keep as long as in
the vicinity of New York and Boston; while, at the same
time, the most delicate grapes of Portugal and Italy are per-
fectly hardy, and ripen their fruit in the greatest perfection.
Good raisins have been made here from such grapes.

"Among all the varied climates of California, there are few
that can claim precedence over Georgetown. Being on a
dividing ridge, it is seldom visited by untimely frosts—the
temperature rarely sinking below 30° in Winter or rising
above 90° in Summer. The atmosphere is so clear and dry
that the mildew or the rot can never visit the grape or the
apple, and, to crown all, there is an abundance of clear, pure
water, winding along the very summit of the country, coming
direct from the perennial fountains which are fed by the snowy
summits to the eastward." To show the interest taken in the
raising of hay and grain, the planting of orchards and vineyards, it is only necessary to ride about a circuit of a few
miles in this locality to be satisfied that those pursuits will
soon become, if not already, the predominant interest in this
neighborhood. We name those most prominent: E. Harkness & Son, W. H. Pratt, Mr. Hotchkiss, A. Lee, Holmes &
Porter, Sands Bros., D. B. Craig, J. F. Richardson, Mrs.
Carlock, Thompson & McConnell, J. Abbee, Bixby & Palmer,
and S. P. Nye. Wheat has been raised in small lots, suffi-
cient to prove that it can be cultivated with success. The
clay lands in some of the valleys around here have produced
a very superior quality of wheat. We took great pleasure in
rambling over the fruit grounds of Messrs. E. Harkness & Son,

half a mile east of Georgetown, and think them worthy of special notice and commendation. Few more enthusiastic cultivators can be found than the elder Harkness, who informs us he has devoted a long life to the cultivation of fruit, and raising fruit trees for sale. Their collection of varieties was brought from Illinois in 1857, and they have been gradually extending their orchards every season since that time. The amount of labor they expend in planting a single tree would astonish most persons. Their terraces along the steep side hills are cut with great labor and with perfect regularity, falling one inch in ten feet, so as to give a gentle flow to water for irrigation. Large excavations are made for each tree, and the hole filled with fine surface soil—about five cubic yards of earth are handled by the spade in planting each tree. Although this system is very expensive in the first instance, it is believed to be the most economical in the end, as it renders irrigation cheap and easy ever after. They have a great variety of various kinds of fruit trees, and several varieties of grapes, all of which have every appearance of a thrifty, healthy growth, and give fine promise of in a few years returning to them large rewards for their money and labor.

A company is now organizing for building of a road, the coming season, from this place to Washoe which, it is confidently expected, will materially increase the business of the town. On a survey of the present situation and future prospects of this place, we are led to believe that there are but few towns that have more to encourage them to hope for a healthy rapid growth than this beautiful mountain town.

CHURCHES.

Methodist Episcopal Church,..............Rev. E. A. Wible
Methodist Episcopal Church, South,......Rev. J. W. Leach

MASONS.

Georgetown Lodge No. 25, was chartered in 1851—
Thomas Wren,.............................Worthy Master
E. L. Crawford..............................Secretary

Georgetown Chapter No. 25, R. A. M.—
Thomas Wren,..............................High Priest
Richard Doncaster,...........................Secretary

I. O. OF O. F.

Memento Lodge No. 37; instituted 1855—
Z. Pierce,.................................Noble Grand
J. L. Atkinson,.....................Recording Secretary

AMERICAN HOUSE,

FORMERLY ORLEANS HOTEL,

Orleans Street, between Main and Church Streets,

GEORGETOWN.

SAMUEL CURRIER.................... PROPRIETOR.

☞ Having leased the above well known and favorite House, and put it in excellent condition for the accommodation of visitors, would be pleased to wait on all who may favor him with their patronage.

RALPH BALMFORTH,

GEORGETOWN

LIVERY, FEED, SALE AND EXCHANGE STABLE,

Main Street, adjoining the Union Hotel.

Exchange with Squires & Bayler, Placerville.

SADDLE HORSES AND BUGGIES

Furnished on the shortest notice.

GEORGETOWN DIRECTORY.

A

Alden Samuel, druggist, with P. W. Cunningham.
Andrews Thomas, miner, east side Church street.
Andrews James, cabinet maker, east side Church street.
AMERICAN HOTEL, corner Church and Orleans streets.
Ash Robert, clerk, with Glassman & Forrester.
ASHTON JOHN, saloon keeper, east side Main street.
Asher S., clerk, with Bloom, west side Main street.
Atkinson J. L., miner, south side Main street.
Ault William, east side Church street.

B

Baldwin Mrs., residence, Union Hotel.
BALMFORTH RALPH, livery stable, east side Main street.
Bell Aaron, miner, east side Main street.
Bellows R. H., sashmaker, west side Church street.
Benjamin William, saddler, east side Main street.
Berry S. A., carpenter west side Main street.
Bixby William, farmer, east side Placer street.
Blackwell John A., attorney, east side Main street.
Bloom S., merchant, west side Main street.
Bonnefauir Louis, west side Church street.
BRADY H. J., Main street.

Bowker John, laborer, east side Church street.
Bradbury T., miner, west side Church street.
Bradly H., J. liquor dealer, east side Main street.
BURRNIE A., merchant tailor, west side Main street.
Bryant Lewis, miner.
Burr & Spencer, dentists, west side Church street.
Burr James, of B. & S., west side Church street.
Burnham O. H., merchant, foot of Main street.
Buchler John, miner.

C

Carpenter J. G., lawyer, east side Main street.
Carpenter Thomas, oyster saloon, east side Main street.
Catholic Church, west side Church street.
Chitwood Wiley, speculator, east side Main street.
Clark Charles, butcher, east side Main street.
Cook George, teamster, east side Main street.
Conness John, east side Placer street.
Cummings William, east side Church street.
CUNNINGHAM P. W., merchant, west side Main street.
CURRIER SAMUEL, proprietor American Hotel.

D

Davis James, miner; boards at Robinett's.
Dever John, boards at Robinett's.
Dever D. O., clerk, with Jackson, west side Main street.
Downs A., farmer, east side Main street.

E

Eastman & Williams, attorneys, east side Main street.
Eastman J. G.. of E. & W., residence, Union Hotel.

F

Fairhurst G. W., blacksmith, east side Main street.
Ferguson Robert, miner, west side Church street.
Foley Thomas, laborer.
Forrester James, of Glassman & Forrester, w. s. Main st.
Fountain G., livery stable, west side Main street.
Fuller Hiram, of Jerrett & Fuller, east side Main street.
Fredericch C., physician, west side Main street.

G

Gates John, teamster, west side Main street.
Gibbs W. T,, blacksmith, east side Church street.
Gill Martin, restaurant, west side Main street.
Gill Hiram, blacksmith, east side Main street.
GLASSMAN & FORRESTER, merchants, w. s. Main st.
Glassman Jacob, of G. & F., west side Main street.
Goldstien Jacob, merchant, west side Main street.
Graham Francis, stock dealer, Sacramento street.
Griffith John, painter, west side Main street.

H

Haddix I., miner, west side Main street.
Harkness & Son, nursery.
HARKNESS EDSON, of Harkness & Son.
Harkness R., of Harkness & Son.
HARDEN J. B., proprietor Union Hotel, e. s. Main street.
Hart William, merchant, west side Main street.
Hamilton Henry, butcher, east side Main street.
Harmon John, laborer, east side Main street.
Heacock H., laborer, west side Church street.
Hulford E., stage driver.

Hussey James, constable, east side Main street.
Hussey George, carpenter, east side Main street.
HYATT A. A., clerk, in Spear's Bank, west side Main street.

I

Ingham Samuel, Deputy Collector.
I. O. O. F. Hall, west side Main street.

J

JACKSON S. J. & BRO., merchants, west side Main street.
Jackson S. J., of S. J. Jackson & Bro.
Jackson M., of S. J. Jackson & Bro.
Jacobs E., merchant, west side Main street.
Jacobs S., merchant, west side Main street.
JACOBS HENRY, merchant and postmaster, w. s. Main st.
Jerrett & Fuller, livery stable, east side Main street.
Jerrett Daniel, of J. &. F., east side Main street.
Jones E., miner, east side Main street.

K

Karpstein Charles, butcher, east side Main street.
Keefer W., fruit grower, west side Church street.
Knox Shannon, carpenter, west side Main street.
KOHN H. No. 2, dry goods and clothing, w. s. Main street.

L

Leach Rev. J. W. pastor M. E. Church South.
Labner L., clerk, with H. Kohn.
Lovinski Bros., grocers, west side Main street.
Lusk Mrs. D., milliner and dressmaker, west side Main st.,
Lyons Hiram, teamster; boards at Robinett's.

PROUT & STAHLMAN,

FIRST-CLASS BARBER SHOP,

GEORGETOWN. CAL.

HOT AND COLD BATHS.

JOHN I. SPEAR, JR.,

BANKER,

GEORGETOWN.

CHECKS ON SAN FRANCISCO.

P. W. CUNNINGHAM,

—— DEALER IN ——

BOOKS, STATIONERY, WALL PAPER, COAL OIL,

LAMPS, ETC., ETC.,

DRUGS, CHEMICALS, PATENT MEDICINES,

Glass, Oils, Paints, Varnishes, Perfumery,
Fancy Goods, etc.,

CORNER OF MAIN AND PLACER STREETS,

GEORGETOWN.

M

Mangold G., baker, east side Main street.

Masonic Hall, west side Main street.

McCOY JAMES, merchant, corner Orleans and Main sts.

McCormick F., teamster, west side Church street.

McKENNEY D. C., of Pilot Creek Water and Mining Co.

Millette E., restaurant, west side Main street.

Miller Jacob, baker, east side Main street.

Miners' Hotel, west side Main street.

Morgan M., saloon keeper, east side Main street.

Morgan Mrs. F., east side Main street.

Morse G. W., shoemaker, east side Main street.

Murphy Richard, miner.

Murray John, blacksmith, east side Church street.

O

Oboy Michael, miner.

Odenheimer William, shoemaker, west side Main street.

Orelly Charles, merchant, east side Church street.

Owen Nelson, blacksmith, east side Church street.

P

PARKER & WELLINGTON, stage proprietors, office at
    Union Hotel.

Parsons George, saloon keeper, east side Main street.

Pearson Thomas, farmer.

Pease E. R., school teacher ; boards at Union Hotel.

Pierce Z., Supervisor 3d District.

Porter A. W., road overseer.

Porter H. M., miner, east side Church street.

Pratt E., miner ; boards at Bryant's.

PROUT & STAHLMAN, barbers, west side Main street.
Prout C. H., of P. & S., west side Main street.
Pilot Creek Water and Mining Co.

R

Reese F., watchmaker, west side Main street.
Richie George, butcher, east side Main street.
ROBINETT E., proprietor Miners' Hotel, west side Main st.
Russell Hiram, shoemaker, at McCoy's.

S

Schooley William, butcher, east side Main street.
Schneider William, brewer.
Shanklin J. W., of Woodside & Co.; lumber dealers.
Shephard B., saddler, with Benjamin.
Shirly F., saloon keeper, east side Main street.
Silva F., teamster, east side Main street.
SPEAR JOHN I. Jr., banker, west side Main street.
Spencer W. E., of Burr & S., dentist, west side Church st.
Stanton Thomas E., teamster.
Stahlman W., of Prout & Stahlman, barber, w. s. Main st.
Stegall H., saloon keeper, west side Church steeet.
Stemmitz ——, baker, west side Church street.
Stevens William, west side Church street.
Stevens James, butcher, west side Main street.
STONE W. H. & Co., of Pilot Creek Water and Mining Co.
Stone W. H., residence, El Dorado street.
Stout John, clerk at McCoy's.
SWARTZ & Co., bakers, south side Main street.
Swartz D., of S. & Co., baker, east side Main street.
SWIFT JOSEPH, soda and liquor dealer, foot of Main st.

T

Taylor Samuel, laborer, east side Main street.
Tell William, butcher, west side Main street.
Thomas W. L., physician, office at Union Hotel.
Town Hall, corner Church and Orleans streets.
Turner Jared, physician and druggist, west side Main street.

U

Union Hotel, I. B. Hardin proprietor, east side Main street.
Uhlfelter Henry, clerk with H. Kohn.

V

Viard Virginia, milliner, east side Main street.

W

Watson E. H., ditch agent, El Dorado street.
Wader E., teamster.
Wells, Fargo & Co., express office, west side Main street.
Wells Mrs. Harriet, dress maker, west side Church street.
West Robert, saloon keeper, west side Main street.
White Joseph, saloon keeper, east side Church street.
Wible Rev. E. A., pastor M. E. Church.
Williams J. J., lawyer, of E. & W., office east side Main st.
Williams Jonah, barkeeper, Miners' Hotel.
Williams J., clerk, with Jackson & Bro.
WOODSIDE & Co., lumber dealers, east side Main street.
Woodside Milton, of W. & Co., east side Main street.
Wren Thomas, surveyor, east side Church street.

GLASSMAN & FORRESTER,

FIRE-PROOF BRICK BUILDING, MAIN STREET,

GEORGETOWN,

——Wholesale and Retail Dealers in——

𝕻rovisions, 𝕲roceries,

Liquors, Flour, Grain, Cigars, Crockery, Hardware, Glassware, Stoves, Tinware, and all kinds of

PRODUCE.

☞ All orders promptly attended to.   Terms—CASH.

PLACERVILLE REPUBLICAN
NEWSPAPER,
𝕭ook and 𝕵ob 𝕻rinting
ESTABLISHMENT.
(OFFICE, IN SEBASTOPOL HALL.)

BOOK AND JOB PRINTING

Neatly, cheaply and expeditiously executed at the Office of

The Placerville Republican,

PLACERVILLE.

PART V.

—

COLOMA.

NEW ESTABLISHMENT.

COLOMA RESTAURANT,

Main Street, Coloma.

WINTERMANTEL & BROTHER - - PROPRIETORS.

The increase of our business has compelled us to establish the above Restaurant. This place is conducted on the European plan, viz: Open day and night; Meals at all hours; Single Meals or Board by the day or week; Board with or without Lodging.

The TABLE will always be supplied with all the delicacies of the Season. As this is one of the finest Restaurants in the State, and as our Table shall always contain the best, we promise to please all who call on us. We are also prepared to furnish, at the shortest notice, for Balls, Parties, etc., all kinds of Plain and Ornamental **Confectionery, Cakes and Pies.** The BASEMENT of this Restaurant contains a BAR, supplied with the best of Liquors, Wines, Lager Beer, etc., to be obtained in the State. A fine BILLIARD TABLE for those who are fond of the game.

THE MINERS' HOTEL, established by us in 1849, will be kept open as formerly, and the patronage given to us for the last twelve years we will endeavor to merit in future.

EL DORADO BREWERY,

MAIN STREET, COLOMA.

☞ The undersigned, having completed one of the finest Cellars in the State, are now prepared to furnish BETTER LAGER than has heretofore been made in this place. Their improved facilities enable them to defy competition in price, quality or quantity. Complete satisfaction guaranteed.

WINTERMANTEL & BROTHER.

HISTORY OF COLOMA.

The town of Coloma has obtained a world-wide notoriety, from its having been the place where gold was first discovered in this State, by the American people. One cannot view this valley, from any of its surrounding hills, without feeling that the " glittering dust " which we are all striving to obtain, was discovered in a most beautiful place. Neither can we pass from point to point and view the work of those who only sought for golden treasures, and then left, leaving an upturned and defaced surface as the only evidence of their presence, without feeling a sense of relief as we turn and witness the many comfortable and beautiful homes to be seen all around, upon the hill sides, and nestling in the quiet valleys about, showing evidences of civilization and refinement on every side. It is gratifying to know that if the gold-seeker and his occupation should pass away from this locality, that there is every probability that it will become as much renowned for its fine varieties of fruit, its extensive vineyards, its rich and delicious wines, and superior brandies, as for its having been the place where gold was first discovered. This place has so far escaped the ravages of a general conflagration ; in that respect, being more fortunate than most towns in California. In other respects it has had its prosperous and its adverse times. On the first organization of El Dorado county, it was made the shire-town, and so remained for several years. It supported a large population and did a great business, and for a long time remained the principal place in the county. After the removal of the county seat, and the decline of mining operations in its vicinity, its prominence as a place of business began to decline, until, at this time, it is more noted for its good society, handsome family residences, its churches and schools, than for the extent of its business. It seems probable that at this time it has reached its lowest ebb, and that it will now continue to advance, as new channels of business are prosecuted and developed, until it will far surpass all former greatness.

We think it was in this place that the plan of obtaining water, for mining purposes, by artificial means, was first put into successful operation. The first ditch for mining purposes was known as the El Dorado Ditch, on the south bank of the river, and six miles in extent. This property paid large dividends to its owners, and induced the construction of many more for the same objects—the principal ones being the Hollingsworth & Co. Ditch, on the north bank of the river; the Coloma Canal, also on the north bank of the river; the Shanghac Ditch, upon the south bank; the Williams Ditch, upon the north bank; the Greenhorn Ditch, upon the south bank, and the U. S. M. Ditch, upon the north bank of the river,—the last being the largest of any. It is said all of these ditches were profitable investments to their owners, and of immense benefit to the miners and agriculturalists in this vicinity.

Upon the decline of mining operations in this locality many persons engaged in the business of planting orchards and vineyards, the pleasing result of which is seen in the many beautiful homes which adorn this pleasant valley. Among the most noted gardens and orchards upon the north side of the river may be mentioned those of Messrs. E. Woodruff and A. A. Van Guelder—the latter with a foresight which does him much credit, was one of the first to engage in the planting and raising of a variety of fruit and grapes,

the result attained has far exceeded the expectations of the
most sanguine. The principal fruit growers upon the south
side of the river are Henry Mahler, Jonas Wilder, Henry
Pierce, Edward Delory, Hon. T. H. Williams, H. Hawley,
John Alhoff, J. G. Vanderheyden, John Crocker and Mrs.
C. M. Robertson ; many of these also pay considerable attention to the planting of vineyards and manufacture of wine.
Among those who devote their principal attention to vine
growing and the manufacture of wine and brandy, are Martin
Alhoff, Jonas Wilder, and Mrs. C. M. Robertson, who have
already acquired a reputation which places them in the front
rank among those capable of judging of their merits. If
any preference is given to either, it would be to Martin Alhoff
for his wines, and to Mrs. Robertson for her very superior
brandy. Mr. J. W. Marshall, renowned for having been the
first discoverer of gold at this place, on the 19th of January
1848, has planted upon the hill sides near this place an extensive vineyard of choice varieties, which promises to return
him a rich reward for his labors.

Mr. Robert Chalmers may be quoted, not only as a model
landlord, but as the model farmer of this place, as, in addition
to quite an extensive orchard and garden, he has the best
breed of hogs, the best blooded stock, and the largest field in
grain of any farmer in this locality. This place has a Lodge
of Masons and one of Odd Fellows. Three quite good church
buildings, occupied by M. E. Church, the Episcopalian Church
and the Catholic Church.

CHURCHES.

Emanuel Church, (Episcopalian.) organized Sept. 15th. 1856—
Rev. C. .C Peirce, Pastor.

Methodist Episcopal Church, organized by Rev. Isaac Owen,
in 1850. Services every Sabbath, by the Pastor. Rev. W
N. Smith.

First Baptist Church, organized by Rev. O. C. Wheeler, Oct.. 1856. No regular stated preaching at present.

Catholic Church, organized in 1858. Services, by Rev. James Largan, on the third Sabbath of each month.

MASONS.

Acacia Lodge No. 92, F. and A. M. Instituted at Coloma Nov. 1st, 1855. Meets the Thursday of or next preceding the full moon in each month—

J. B. Maxey,...............................Worthy Master
J. G. Canfield................................Secretary

I. O. OF O. F.

Coloma Lodge No. 27, I. O. O. F., was organized August 21st, 1854. Meets every Saturday evening—

J. G. Vanderheyden,.......................Noble Grand
S. W. Weller,.......................Recording Secretary

COLOMA DIRECTORY.

A

ALHOFF MARTIN, wine-maker, west side Sacramento st.
Alhoff John, gardener, west side Sacramento street.
Allen Robert, clerk, with R. Bell.
Armory Coloma Greys, south side Main street.

B

Barry Mrs., laundress, north side Main street.
Bekeart Frank, gunsmith, north side Main street.
BELL ROBERT, merchant, north side Main street.
Bird Frank, stage driver; boards at Sierra Nevada House.
BRAMER F., carpenter, south side Main street.
Brockway Henry, tailor, south side Main street.
Brown J. C., merchant, south side Main street.

C

CANFIELD & Co., J. G., merchants, north side Main st.
Canfield J G., of J. G. C. & Co.; residence, w. s. Jail street.
Catholic Church, south side Church street.
CHALMERS ROBERT, proprietor Sierra Nevada House,
    north side Main street.
CHALMERS GEORGE, merchant south side Main street.
Clark R. V., butcher, south side Main street.
Clark James M., saloon keeper, north side Main street.
Cooper M., clerk, with E. Weller, north side Main street.

Cox Rodger, farmer.
Coloma Theater. south side Main street.
Crocker John, teamster, south side Howell street.
CURTIS JOHN, constable, south side Main street.

D

DAVIS L., baker, south side Main street.
Day Henry, harness maker, north side Main street.
Delory E., fruit grower, south side Main street.
Douglas George A., Justice of the Peace, s. s. Main street.
Duffy James, west side Sacramento street.

E

EICHELROTH W., physician and surgeon, n. s. Main st.
ENGLEBRECHT P., billiard saloon, north side Main street.
Episcopal Church, south side Church street.

F

Fleming Martin, laundry, south side Main street.
Fowler T. B., toll bridge, Bridge street.
Fox Philo, teamster, south side Main street.

G

COLOMA GREYS, Captain, J. G Vanderheyden ; 1st.
    Lieutenant, S. B. Weller ; 2d Lieutenant, George O.
    Kies ; Brevet 2d Lieutenant, S. H Brockway. Num-
    ber of members, 41.

H

Hanks James, east side Sacramento street.
Hawley H., fruit grower, west side Jail street.
Holmes Mrs., school teacher, east side Sacramento street.
Hollingsworth W. F., lumber dealer, west side Jail street.

J

Jones W. A., saloon keeper, south side Main street.
Jones & Castile, saloon keepers, south side Main street.

K

Kies George O., printer, south side Main street.
Kimball O., of J. G. C. & Co., merchant, n. s. Main st.
Knopt, M., saloon keeper, south side Main street.

L

Lathrop S., jeweler, south side Main street.
LEVY J.. merchant, south side Main street.
Lonzamsky H., clerk, with J. Levy, south side Main street.

M

Mahler Henry, fruit grower, south side Howell street.
Marshall J. W., gold discoverer, south side Church street.
Masonic Hall, south side Main street.
Methodist E. Church, east side Sacramento street.
Merrill Charles E., livery, north side Main street.
Merrill Bros., meat market, north side Main streett
Merrill O., of M. Bros., north side Main street.
Merrill A., of M. Bros., north side Main street.
Miller John, steward, at Sierra Nevada House.
Miller E., with C. E. Merrill, livery.
Miller George, saloon keeper, south side Main street.
McBride B., saloon keeper, south side Main street.
McDonald J. H,, laborer.
Mitchell Paul, express and telegraph agent, s. s. Main st.
Myers H., teamster, south side Main street.

N

Nuss & Co., brewers, Brewery street.
Nicholls Mrs., south side Main street.

O

Odd Fellows' Hall, south side Main street.
Oliver G. B., saloon keeper, south side Main street.
Osborn R., blacksmith, north side Main street.

P

Parker J. W., stage agent ; boards at Sierra Nevada House.
Patrick James, miner; north side Main street.
Pierce Henry, nurseryman, south side Church street.
Porter Frank, stage driver; boards at Sierra Nevada House.

R

Robertson Mrs. C. M., Victoria Gardens, e. s. Sacramento st.

S

Scheiffer Charles, saloon keeper, south side Main street.
Scogin William, carpenter, south side Main street.
Seely Joseph, jeweler, east side Jail street.
Smallwood J. A., barber, south side Main street.
Smith W. N., pastor M. E. Church, south side Sacramento st.
Smith E. M. farmer, west side Sacramento street.
Storer John, carpenter, south side Main street.
Sullivan Thomas, watchman, south side Main street.

T

Teuscher John, miner, south side Howell street.
Trescott J. C., stage proprietor, west side Jail street
Trimble John, gardener, west side Bridge street.

V

Vanderheyden J. G., gardener, west side Jail street.
Van Guelder A. A., lawyer, east side Bridge street.

W

Weller E., merchant, north side Main street.
Weller S. B., clerk, with E. Weller, north side Main street.
Weiner ——, clerk, with Morris, south side Main street.
Williams Abner, shoemaker, north side Main street.
Williams George, lawyer, west side Sacramento street.
Wilder Jonas, gardener, south side Main street.
Winter Samuel, wagon maker, north side Main street.
WINTERMANTEL & BRO., hotel and brewery, north
    side Main street.
Wintermantel L., of W. & Bro., north side Main street.
Wintermantel T., of W. & Bro., north side Main street.
Wixon P., laborer, west side Sacramento street.
Woodruff E., farmer, North Coloma.
Woodruff A., farmer, North Coloma.